Lecture Notes
in Economics and
Mathematical Systems

Managing Editors: M. Beckmann and W. Krelle

254

Sigrid Müller

Arbitrage Pricing of Contingent Claims

Springer-Verlag
Berlin Heidelberg New York Tokyo

Author

Dr. Sigrid Müller
Institut für Gesellschafts- und Wirtschaftswissenschaften
der Universität Bonn
Adenauerallee 24–42, D-5300 Bonn 1, FRG

ISBN-13: 978-3-540-15973-5 e-ISBN-13: 978-3-642-46560-4
DOI: 10.1007/978-3-642-46560-4

Meinen Eltern

PREFACE

This book is intended as a contribution to the theory of contingent claim valuation based on arbitrage considerations. It is concerned with preference-free valuations of contingent claims (such as options written on a stock) in frictionless multiperiod securities markets that do not permit arbitrage profits. Besides the question of pricing it considers the possibility of hedging in securities markets.

The research reported in this book was carried out at the Institut für Gesellschafts- und Wirtschaftswissenschaften, University of Bonn. While working in this field and preparing this monograph I received helpful comments and encouragement from many people, and I would like to thank all of them. Special thanks are due to Prof.Dr.Dieter Sondermann. He first stimulated my interest in the theory of contingent claim valuation and commented on my work at various stages. Furthermore, I would like to thank Profs. Martin Hellwig, Peter Schönfeld and Klaus Schürger, all University of Bonn, for helpful comments on earlier versions of this monograph. Parts of this monograph were presented at various meetings including the European Meeting of the Econometric Society, Pisa 1983, the European Meeting of the Econometric Society, Madrid 1984, and the third Conference "Geld, Banken und Versicherungen", Karlsruhe 1984. I greatly appreciate comments of Profs. Stephen Ross, Yale University, and Michael Brennan, UCLA. I take this opportunity to express my indebtness to my colleague Dr.Shinichiro Nakamura for his constant encouragement during the laborious process of writing this monograph.

Finally, I gratefully acknowledge the financial support of Deutsche Forschungsgemeinschaft at the Sonderforschungsbereich 303, University of Bonn, which enabled me to prepare the present monograph.

Sigrid Müller

CONTENTS

1 Introduction

Along with the successful introduction of listed options at international stock exchanges the interest in the valuation of options or generally in contingent claim pricing grew rapidly. Contingent claim pricing as opposed to general financial pricing theory studies the problem of valuing financial assets, whose value is explicitly dependent on the exogenously given value of some underlying asset. The most prominent example is a European call option written on a stock. Since it represents the right to buy the stock at a specified price and date, the value of the option at this date depends on the value of the stock.

Associated with contingent claim pricing is the question of hedging, i.e. making counterbalancing investments with regard to certain kinds of risk in order to reduce or completely eliminate such sources of uncertainty. Hedging is of increasing importance taking into account the growing number of newly established securities such as puts and calls on spot exchange or currency option bonds. It might be a suitable means to substantially reduce the risk exposure resulting from heavy fluctuations on financial markets.

The theory of contingent claim valuation is concerned with the following questions. Is there a price for every contingent claim, which given the prices of the underlying assets does not permit arbitrage profits? If so, is this price unique and independent of preferences of investors? How could one actually determine such preference-free valuations for specific contingent claims? What are the implications of those prices on hedging? These and related questions are studied in the present book in a unified framework.

Before briefly summarizing the main results, a few remarks on the approach taken are in order. This monograph is concerned with preference-free valuation of contingent claims in a frictionless multiperiod securities market model, where trading in the given securities takes place continuously. The question of existence and uniqueness of preference-free valuations of contingent claims is addressed under the assumption that the securities markets considered do not permit arbitrage profits. The analysis is performed in terms of trading strategies in the given securities. Trading strategies are determined that might be of interest for the purpose of hedging.

The greatest stimulus for the theory of contingent claim valuation grew out of the paper by BLACK/SCHOLES (1973) on the pricing of a European call option. BLACK/SCHOLES derive a valuation formula for a European call option in a frictionless securities market model with a riskless bond and the stock, where trading in the bond and the stock takes place continuously. The valuation principle employed is essentially the following. One determines a continuously adjusted portfolio in the bond and the stock that produces exactly the same pattern of cash-flows as the option and that apart from the initial investment neither requires funds to be invested nor allows for withdrawals. Such a portfolio is called self-financing. Assuming absence of arbitrage opportunities, there is a unique price for the option, namely the initial investment in the self-financing portfolio that produces the same cash-flows as the option. Although the basic idea of this valuation principle is rather simple, there are problems associated with it, which will be elaborated on in Chapter 2.

Chapter 2 serves two purposes. First, it surveys the literature on contingent claim valuation with special emphasis on preference-free approaches to the valuation of contingent claims. Secondly, it elaborates on the problems associated with the approaches to be found in the literature and thus introduces some of the questions to be dealt with in the present monograph.

Chapter 3 introduces the basic model of a two-date economy with uncertainty with initial date zero and final date T. There are (K+1) securities that allow for substitution of time zero consumption for time T consumption. We examine the decision problem of an agent concerning his present consumption and state contingent future consumption by means of a trading strategy in securities. Prices of securities are considered realizations of a continuous-time stochastic process. First of all, agents' trading is restricted to a finite number of prespecified trading dates. Agents employ simple self-financing trading strategies, i.e. trading strategies depending only on past prices of securities and neither requiring nor generating funds between the initial and the final date, when rearranging the portfolio at the given finite set of trading dates. A simple self-financing trading strategy gives rise to or generates a contingent claim at the final date, a simply attainable contingent claim. If there are no simple arbitrage opportunities, there is a unique price for every simply attainable contingent claim, which is independent of agents' preferences. This price is given by the initial investment associated with the simple self-financing generating trading strategy. It is examined whether the so defined price system on the space of simply attainable contingent claims has a "well-behaved" extension. Necessary and sufficient conditions for the existence of a price system on the space of contingent claims that is consistent with the price process of the given securities are given. A consistent price system can be described by means of an equivalent martingale measure. Equivalent martingale measures can be interpreted as different subjective probability measures that agents of the class considered may have.

Chapter 4 extends the model described in Chapter 3 to the continuous-time trading case, i.e. agents may rearrange their portfolios at every time t between the initial and the final date. A continuous-time self-financing trading strategy is defined as the limit of a sequence of simple self-financing trading strategies with respect to a certain norm introduced on the space of all continuous-time trading strategies. This norm takes into account both gains or losses due to price changes and funds to be invested or to withdraw that are associated with a trading strategy. A continuous-time self-financing trading strategy is characterized by a stochastic integral representation of the associated value process. It is shown that a contingent claim is generated by a self-financing trading strategy if and only if it is the limit in mean square of a sequence of simply attainable contingent claims. These results are applied to the classical BLACK/SCHOLES model, yielding the BLACK/SCHOLES formula. The BLACK/SCHOLES formula gives the value of a European call option written on a stock, the price process of which is specified as a geometric Brownian motion with exercise price K and expiration date T. In this monograph the BLACK/SCHOLES formula will be derived without the standard assumption of a functional relationship

$$O_t = f(t, S_t^1)$$

between the option price O_t and the stock price S_t^1 at time t, where f is a twice continuously differentiable function. A self-financing generating trading strategy is determined as well as an approximating sequence of simple self-financing trading strategies. These considerations might be of interest for hedging purposes as well as for empirical studies. Then a characterization of contingent claims that are generated by continuous-time self-financing trading strategies is given. It is shown that a contingent claim is generated by a self-financing trading strategy if and only if it has constant expectation with respect to all P-continuous signed martingale measures. This characterization yields explicit valuation formulas for specific contingent claims and solves the problem of dependence on agents' preferences. For specific security price processes the classes of contingent claims that can be generated by means of self-financing trading strategies are determined and valuation formulas are obtained. Then we bridge the gap between the valuation method proposed in this monograph and the valuation method by means of difference-differential equations to be found in the literature. It has to be emphasized, however ,that the valuation method proposed in this monograph is the more general one. Special attention will be given to complete securities market models. A securities market model is complete, if every contingent claim can be generated by a self-financing trading strategy in the given securities. It is shown that a securities market model is complete if and only if the set of equivalent martingale measures is singleton. By means of counterexamples we determine those assumptions that are indispensable for the results of Chapter 4 to obtain.

Chapter 5 deals with extensions of the classical BLACK/SCHOLES model. In order to apply the theory developed in Chapter 4 we have to transform the extended BLACK/SCHOLES model to be analysed. A discounted securities market model is considered and an equivalent martingale measure for the discounted security price process is determined. We examine the relationship between the original and the transformed model. It is shown that the results of the discounted securities market model carry over to the original model provided that the bond price process S^0 as well as its inverse $(S^0)^{-1}$ are semimartingales. The extended BLACK/SCHOLES model is shown to be complete and a self-financing generating trading strategy is determined in the case of a European call option. Again this is achieved without any kind of differentiability assumption. Furthermore, possible sources of incompleteness for generalized BLACK/SCHOLES models are listed.

Chapter 6 shows the limitations of the preference-free approach to the valuation of contingent claims introduced in Chapter 4 by means of a simple example. If one considers the BLACK/SCHOLES model with the only exception that the variance parameter of the underlying stock price process changes, say, according to the outcome of an election, the contingent claim associated with a European call option on this stock cannot be generated by a self-financing trading strategy in the bond and the stock. The possibility of generating the option by trading strategies that are not self-financing is discussed. Several generating trading strategies are found and their associated gains or losses are calculated. It is examined whether there is a "best" generating trading strategy. A trading strategy is determined that has smallest expected squared gains or losses among all generating trading strategies. The expected gains or losses associated with this trading strategy are zero. The initial investment associated with this optimal trading strategy gives a special consistent price for the option.

Chapter 7 presents concluding remarks and suggestions for future research.

In the Appendix mathematical notions and facts are collected in such a way as to make this monograph self-contained.

2 The Valuation of Contingent Claims: A Survey

This chapter surveys the literature on contingent claim valuation. Special emphasis will be given to models that do not assume specific preferences of investors. As far as it is needed in this introductory chapter, a unified framework for the valuation of contingent claims is introduced more or less informally.

The major part of the literature on contingent claim valuation is concerned with option pricing. Only recently more complex contingent claims have been considered. A common feature of all models is a kind of *no-arbitrage assumption*. *Arbitrage* is the "buying of bills of exchange, stocks etc. in one market and selling them at a profit in another market" (Webster's New World Dictionary (1978)). Because of the no-arbitrage assumption, one often refers to these models as *Arbitrage Pricing Models*. Even though models based on the *Capital Asset Pricing* approach due to SHARPE (1964), LINTNER (1965) and MOSSIN (1966) may also include a lack-of-arbitrage-opportunities assumption (cf. CHAMBERLAIN/ROTHSCHILD (1983)), this approach will not be considered in this monograph.

The valuation of contingent claims is based on the microeconomic theory of investment under uncertainty. There are K+1 investment opportunities called *securities*. Trading in these securities, which are often called *basic securities*, is possible at certain trading dates. The set of trading dates is denoted by $\mathcal{T}$. $\mathcal{T} = \{0,\dots,T\}, T \in \mathbb{N}$, represents the discrete-time T-period case, whereas $\mathcal{T} = [0,T]$, $T \in \mathbb{R}_{++}$, represents the continuous-time case, where trading in the basic securities is possible at every date $t \in [0,T]$. The prices at which the basic securities are being traded are considered realizations of stochastic processes S^k, $k \in \{0,\dots,K\}$, on a probability space $(\Omega,\mathcal{F},P)$. S^k is called the *security price process* corresponding to security k. Elements ω of Ω are interpreted as possible states of the world. Thus the real number $S_t^k(\omega)$ gives the price of security k at time t if the state of the world is ω.

• A *contingent claim* is a $\mathcal{F}$-measurable mapping $X : \Omega \to \mathbb{R}$. The most prominent examples of contingent claims are the ones associated with options. An *option* is an agreement between two parties, in which one grants the other the right, but not the obligation, to buy designated securities or commodities from or sell them to him under stated conditions. The buyer of a *call option* obtains the right to buy a specified number of shares of the underlying security from the option seller at a specified price, the *exercise* or *striking price*, up to some indicated date, the *expiration date*. For this right the option buyer pays the seller the *premium* or *option price*. If the underlying security can only be bought (or *called away*) at the expiration date, the option is called *European*. An *American call option* allows the underlying security to be called away at any time up to the expiration date. A *put option* gives the buyer the right to sell the underlying security to the option seller at a specified price up to some indicated date. Again one distinguishes *European* and *American put options*. A *riskless security* is a security or a portfolio of securities, the return of which per invested unit over the basic period is known with certainty.

The following assumptions can be found in almost all models (cf. MERTON (1982), p. 603). Markets are *frictionless*, i.e. there are no transaction costs or taxes, and securities are perfectly divisible. There are no *institutional restrictions*, i.e. short-sales of all securities are allowed without restriction. If there is a riskless security, then the borrowing and lending rate coincide. Furthermore there are *no arbitrage opportunities*, i.e. all riskless securities have the same return per unit invested. The usual assumptions on investors include the following. Investors prefer more consumption to less, i.e. preferences of investors are monotone. Investors are price takers. An investor believes that his or her action cannot affect the probability distribution of the security price processes. All investors have the same information. This information is described by a filtration $(F_t)_{t\in T}$. In the existing literature on contingent claim valuation only uncertainty with respect to the prices of the basic securities is allowed for. KREPS (1980) states that phenomena such as differential information, moral hazard, individual uncertainty about future tastes etc. represent uncertainty which is in general not fully reflected in the security price processes. That is why they are excluded. In those cases it can hardly be expected that the model is *complete*, i.e. that there are valuations for all contingent claims:

> "At best, there are complete markets only in uncertainty which is so reflected".
>
> KREPS (1980), p. 49

Different classes of models can be distinguished. Distinctive features are the time structure of the security price processes, investors' preferences and the distributions of the security price processes. Depending on the structure of $\mathcal{T}$, one distinguishes *discrete-time models* ($\mathcal{T} = \{0,\ldots,T\}$, $T \in \mathbb{N}$) and *continuous-time models* ($\mathcal{T} = [0,T]$, $T \in \mathbb{R}_{++}$). Models based solely on the assumptions on investors' preferences introduced so far, are called *preference-free models*. If valuations of contingent claims are derived assuming specific preferences of investors, we speak of *preference-dependent models*. Depending on the necessity to specify the distribution of the security price processes, one distinguishes *distribution-free* and *distribution-dependent models*.[1)]

The *discrete-time, preference- and distribution-free approach* to the valuation of contingent claims has not been dealt with explicitly in the literature.

The *discrete-time, preference-free and distribution-dependent approach* which is identical to the hedge approach (cf. p. 9) has been treated completely in the literature (cf. HARRISON/KREPS (1979), pp. 392, COX/ROSS/RUBINSTEIN (1979), HARRISON/PLISKA (1981), pp. 224). The class of distributions, which allows for preference-free valuations of contingent claims in discrete-time models is very small. So the question remains whether prices of securities can adequately be described by elements of this class.

One might think of enlarging the class of distributions at the cost of imposing specific preferences, which leads to the *discrete-time, preference- and distribution-dependent* approach. But even in this case the question remains, whether prices of securities can at all be represented by discrete-time security price processes. This objection is often met referring to a limit argument (cf. COX/ROSS/RUBINSTEIN (1979), pp. 246). By permanently increasing the number of trading dates one tries to obtain a better description of the actual price processes. But in the limit this argument entails the transition from discrete-time to continuous-time security price processes.

The *continuous-time, preference- and distribution-free approach* has been initiated by MERTON (1973). This approach yields restrictions as

---

1) Different classes of models are considered by BRENNAN (1979). BRENNAN distinguishes the class of continuous-time, preference-free models and the class of discrete-time, preference-dependent models.

well as qualitative results of "rational" pricing formulas of contingent claims under a no-arbitrage assumption. MERTON (1973) derives properties of and a set of restrictions on option pricing formulas from the assumption that investors prefer more to less. His results are distribution- and preference-free and are thus "general consistency criteria" (SMITH (1976), p. 7) for valuation formulas. This approach is attractive because of its distributional independence. But it is not possible to determine a unique pricing formula.

The *continuous-time, preference-free and distribution-dependent approach* to the valuation of contingent claims rests essentially on a kind of *spanning* property of the basic securities:

> "The ability to trade securities frequently can enable a "few" multiperiod securities to span "many" states of nature".
>
> KREPS (1980),p. 1

It goes back to the *hedge* approach of BLACK and SCHOLES (cf. BLACK/SCHOLES (1973), pp. 641). Even though the derivation by BLACK and SCHOLES is not mathematically correct (cf. HARRISON/PLISKA (1981), BERGMAN (1981) and Chapter 5), it gives the basic idea: to generate the contingent claim by means of a selffinancing portfolio in the basic securities.[1)] A portfolio is called *selffinancing* if it neither requires nor generates funds between the initial and the final date when rearranging it. A portfolio *generates a contingent claim* if it produces exactly the same pattern of cash flows as the contingent claim. The valuation principle rests on the following argument. If arbitrage opportunities are excluded, then there is a unique price for every contingent claim that can be generated by a selffinancing portfolio. This price is given by the initial investment in the generating portfolio.

Although the basic idea of the hedge approach is rather simple, there are problems associated with the modeling of these concepts. What is the right definition of a selffinancing portfolio, when trading takes place continuously? What portfolios should be admissible? How should one define a continuous-time arbitrage opportunity? These concepts are introduced only for portfolios that allow for rearranging at a finite number of trading dates.

---

1) BLACK/SCHOLES (1973) derive a pricing formula of a European call option. In deriving this formula they consider a portfolio in the basic stock and the call option and claim that it is selffinancing and riskless. BLACK and SCHOLES try to generate a riskless contingent claim by means of stocks and options.

Portfolios in the basic securities can conveniently be described by trading strategies. So the questions addressed above could be recast in terms of trading strategies.

BLACK and SCHOLES (cf. BLACK/SCHOLES (1973), p. 645) do not explicitly consider trading strategies. Thus they ignore the dependence of the derived pricing formula on the class of admissible trading strategies. MERTON ((1971),p. 379,(1973),p. 164) and MERTON/SAMUELSON (1974),pp. 85, consider continuous-time trading strategies as limits of discrete-time trading strategies in the case of a continuous security price process, but they do not indicate nor examine the class of admissible trading strategies. HARRISON/KREPS (1979), p. 388,bypass the problems described above by introducing a class of *simple* trading strategies, where trading in the basic securities is only possible at a finite number of prespecified trading dates. Since this class of trading strategies is too small to yield valuations of most contingent claims according to the hedge approach, they introduce a concept of *arbitrage pricing*[1)] (cf. HARRISON/KREPS (1979), pp. 382, 387). HARRISON/PLISKA (1981),p.239, define a class of continuous-time selffinancing trading strategies that depend on a fixed equivalent martingale measure. This dependence is crucial if there are several equivalent martingale measures.[2)]

Besides the problem of determining a suitable class of continuous-time trading strategies there are more foundational problems associated with the pricing of contingent claims by means of selffinancing, generating portfolios. An inherent feature of the hedge approach is a kind of *redundancy* as pointed out by HAKANSSON (1979). If a contingent claim can be generated in a selffinancing way by existing securities, the corresponding financial instrument does not enrich the existing financial markets; thus it is *redundant*. With respect to the pricing of contingent claims according to the hedge approach HAKANSSON concludes:

> "So we find ourselves in the awkward position of being able to derive unambiguous values only for redundant assets and unable to value options which do have social value".
>
> HAKANSSON (1979),p. 723

---

1) See Chapter 4 on the relationship between the *arbitrage pricing concept* of HARRISON/KREPS (1979) and the hedge approach in the continuous-time case.

2) See Chapter 4 on the solution to this problem.

In contrast to the redundancy implied by the hedge approach certain financial instruments and in particular options are considered to enrich the existing financial markets and are regarded as a means to decrease risk exposure. As regards the objection of redundancy, it should be noted that there is a close relationship between the problem of redundancy and the concept of continuous-time trading. The impossibility of continuous-time trading is one explanation for the opening of markets in (in models with continuous-time trading possiblities) redundant financial instruments. As will be shown in Chapter 4, the pricing formulas resulting from the hedge approach in a model with continuous-time trading possibilities can be interpreted as limits to which pricing formulas resulting from the hedge approach in more realistic but less mathematically tractable models converge. The limit argument seems reasonable, since in reality there is access to stock exchanges almost always, including the possibility of switching to other stock exchanges.

A further objection to the hedge approach to the valuation of contingent claims concerns the assumed exogeneity of the security price processes.

Despite all objections the hedge approach is a very popular method for the valuation of contingent claims, and the resulting pricing formulas are the formulas usually used in applications. In particular this applies to the pricing formula of a European call option due to BLACK and SCHOLES, called the *BLACK/SCHOLES formula*. BLACK/SCHOLES (1973), p. 644 give the following pricing formula for a European call option, which is written on a stock with price process S^1, expiration date T and exercise price $K \in \mathbb{R}_{++}$ at time $t \in [0,T]$.

$$S_t^1 \, \Phi\left(\frac{\ln \frac{S_t^1}{K} + (r + \frac{\sigma^2}{2})(T - t)}{\sigma \sqrt{T - t}}\right) - K \exp\,(r(t - T))\, \Phi\left(\frac{\ln \frac{S_t^1}{K} + (r - \frac{\sigma^2}{2})(T-t)}{\sigma \sqrt{T - t}}\right)$$

Φ denotes the distribution function of a standard normally distributed random variable. BLACK and SCHOLES assume that there exists a riskless security, the price process of which is given by

$$S_t^o = S_o^o \exp(rt) \quad , \quad 0 \le t \le T \quad ,$$

where S_o^o and r denote positive constants. The stock price process S^1 is assumed to be a geometric Brownian motion with linear drift and linear variance, i.e. it is of the form

$$S_t^1 = S_o^1 \exp(\sigma W_t + (\mu - \frac{1}{2}\sigma^2)t) \quad , \quad 0 \le t \le T \quad ,$$

where S_o^1, μ and σ denote positive constants and W a standardized Brownian motion. In spite of all theoretical achievements and generalizations (see Chapter 5 for possible generalizations), the BLACK/SCHOLES formula remained the most accepted pricing formula in practical work. Its popularity is based on its rather simple structure. With the exception of the variance parameter σ the BLACK/SCHOLES formula includes only observable variables. In particular, it does not comprise variables such as the "expected return of a security" or parameters,which represent investor attitudes towards risk. The determination of the only unobservable parameter, however, is problematical and it is the topic of quite a lot of research (cf. LATANÉ/RENDLEMAN (1976), BOYLE/ ANANTHANARAYANAN (1977), BECKERS (1981), CHRISTIE (1982), MANASTER/ KOEHLER (1982)).

A lot of work is concerned with the relaxation of the rather restrictive assumptions of the BLACK/SCHOLES model. Among others, the assumption of the existence of a riskless security, the no-dividend assumption and the assumption of a constant exercise price were relaxed. MERTON (1973) derives a pricing formula in a model with a stochastic bond process (see Chapter 5 on the problems one encounters in this case). Furthermore, MERTON (1973) relaxes the assumption of dividend-free securities and considers a model with proportional dividend payments. FISCHER (1978) deals with a stochastic exercise price. The pricing formula derived by FISCHER is based on an extended hedge approach. A selffinancing generating portfolio does only exist in an extended model, which results from the given one after having introduced a new security (see Chapter 6 on the effects of this approach).

A problem dealt with in a large part of the literature is the specification of the security price processes. It is the basic component of the model. Whether or not a contingent claim can be generated by a selffinancing portfolio in the basic securities depends essentially on the distribution of the security price processes. Probably the first treatment of the specification problem is due to BACHELIER (1900) (cf. the English translation of his thesis in COOTNER (1964)). BACHELIER specifies the price process of a basic security as Brownian motion. The objection that prices cannot go negative, resulted in the specification of the security price process as geometric Brownian motion by SPRENKLE (1964), BONESS (1964) and SAMUELSON (1965a). This also is the specification that BLACK/SCHOLES (1973) and MERTON (1973) choose in their models. Empirical studies questioned this specification. FIELIETZ (1971) and BONESS/CHEN/JATUSIPITAK (1974) examine whether the increments of the logarithmic prices are indeed stationary. GREENE/ FIELIETZ (1977) reject the lognormality assumption.[1] MANDELBROT (1963) and FAMA (1963) favor a logstable specification in order to account for the large number of outliers. UPTON/SHANNON (1979) examine the empirical validity of the logstability and lognormality assumption. Because of the observed fat tails BLATTBERG/GONEDES (1974) model the distribution of the logarithmic price increments by a symmetric stable and by a Student distribution. The systematic under- or overestimation by the BLACK/SCHOLES formula in empirical studies[2] led to the specification of the security price process as diffusion process with a constant elasticity of variance (cf. BECKERS (1980), ANANTHANARAYANAN/SCHWARTZ (1980)). COX/ROSS (1976b) extend the analysis to jump processes and obtain an option pricing formula in the case of a geometric Poisson process.

While the specification of the security price processes as geometric Brownian motion or geometric Poisson processes guarantees that every contingent claim can be generated by a selffinancing portfolio in the basic securities, this is no longer true even in the case of simple mixtures of these processes. In those cases it is not possible to generate the contingent claim associated with a European call option in a selffinancing way. Notwithstanding, MERTON (1976b) derives an option pricing formula in the case of a mixed diffusion-jump process. He assumes that the risk of infusions or withdrawals of funds associated with a generating portfolio can be diversified. Empirical studies of this kind of security price processes were performed by BALL/TOROUS (1983a,b). BALL/TOROUS (1983a) report estimation results for a stock return process, which is the Bernoulli-mixture of Brownian motion.

---

1) If a security price process is specified as geometric Brownian motion, the increments of the logarithmic prices are normally distributed. This specification is referred to as lognormality assumption. Accordingly, we speak of the logstability assumption if the increments of the logarithmic prices are assumed to be stable distributed etc.

2) Cf. BLACK/SCHOLES (1972), MERTON (1976b), MACBETH/MERVILLE (1979), (1980),GALAI (1983) and COX/RUBINSTEIN (1983). BLACK/SCHOLES (1972) observe an underestimation (overestimation) of the option price in the case of stocks with a high (low) variance. COX/RUBINSTEIN (1983), p. 10 criticize the overestimation of out-of-money near maturity call options in comparison to at-the-money middle maturity call options on the same stock.

BALL/TOROUS (1983b) estimate the parameters of the stock price process considered by MERTON (1976b).

The continuous-time, preference-free and distribution dependent pricing models described so far all make use of the method suggested by BLACK/SCHOLES (1973). Their starting point is a functional relationship between the unknown price process of the contingent claim and the given security price process. Under suitable regularity conditions one derives the stochastic differential of the unknown price process. Choosing a suitable trading strategy this stochastic differential reduces to a partial differential equation or a difference-differential equation. The solution to this equation with the corresponding boundary condition is the pricing formula, one was looking for.

COX and ROSS (1976b) were the first to apply the following intuitive solution technique. They realized that the derivation of the differential equation associated with the unknown option pricing formula is independent of preferences. They argue that a pricing formula derived from any set of preferences consistent with the distributional assumptions will satisfy this equation:

> "In particular, consider a risk neutral world where the expected return on all assets must be the same. In such a world the value of the option ... [is].the discounted expected value ...".
>
> COX/ROSS (1976a),p. 391

Using this intuitive method of valuation COX/ROSS (1976a,b) derive option pricing formulas for price processes specified as diffusion or jump processes. HARRISON/KREPS (1979) take up this intuitive solution technique and give an economic justification of the pricing of a contingent claim by means of its expected value with respect to a special probability measure, namely an equivalent martingale measure. This "fair-game" or martingale property of the security price processes can be found for example in SAMUELSON ((1965a),p. 791,(1965b),p. 785), SPRENKLE (1964),p. 433 and FAMA (1970),p. 385 . Since the model of HARRISON/KREPS (1979) restricts investors' trading to a finite number of prespecified trading dates,HARRISON/PLISKA (1981),(1983) tried to extend it to allow for continuous-time trading possibilities. This was achieved only incompletely and without economic arguments. The pricing of contingent claims based on equivalent martingale measures was extended to take into account arbitrary stochastic processes. JARROW/RUDD (1982) give an approximate option pricing formula in the case of an arbitrary security price process. Of course, the existence of a selffinancing generating portfolio has to be assumed. Starting from the valuation of a contingent claim as its expected value with respect to an equivalent martingale measure, JARROW/RUDD (1982) use a generalized Edgeworth series expansion to derive a pricing formula by means of an approximating distribution and adjustment terms. JARROW/RUDD (1983) also test the option pricing formula obtained.

The hedge approach has also been applied to more complex contingent claims. SMITH (1979) gives a good survey on this topic. Among others, pricing formulas of European put options (BLACK/SCHOLES (1973), p. 647), commodity options and futures contracts (BLACK (1976a), p. 177) as well as warrants and rights (SMITH (1977)) were derived. Quite often it happened that the solution to the differential equation derived could not be given in closed form because of complicated boundary conditions. In those cases a valuation was obtained numerically (cf. BRENNAN/SCHWARTZ (1977b)).

The *continuous-time, preference- and distribution-dependent approach* to the valuation of contingent claims makes use of preference or utility specifications along with assumptions about the distribution of the price processes. Almost all models that were published before the BLACK/SCHOLES model depend on specific preferences or utility functions. A more recent model which is based on this approach is due to RUBINSTEIN (1976). RUBINSTEIN gives a derivation of the BLACK/SCHOLES formula in the case that investors are restricted to trade in the basic securities at a finite number of trading dates.

3 Existence of Consistent Price Systems

This chapter is concerned with the existence of consistent price systems on the space of contingent claims within the framework of a partial equilibrium model. A two-date economy with uncertainty is considered in Section 3.1, and the decision problem of an agent concerning his present consumption and state contingent future consumption by means of a trading strategy in securities is stated. Section 3.2 introduces the basic "no-arbitrage" assumption and gives necessary and sufficient conditions for the existence of a price system on the space of contingent claims that is consistent with the price process of the given securities. A consistent price system can be described by means of an equivalent martingale measure. This section closely follows the reasoning of HARRISON/ KREPS (1979). Section 3.3 gives models that possess at least one equivalent martingale measure.

3.1 The basic model

An economy with uncertainty will be considered, which covers two periods, t=0 and t=T. A probability space $(\Omega,\mathcal{F},P)$ is given, where elements ω of Ω represent states of the world. For reasons of simplification a single consumption good, the *numeraire*, is considered. This is feasible, since the question to be addressed is the investment decision of an individual not his choice of consumption. Investors or agents are interested in certain consumption at date zero and state contingent consumption at time T. A *consumption plan* is defined by a scalar c_0 at time zero and by a contingent claim X at time T, i.e. a $\mathcal{F}$-measurable random variable. $X(\omega)$ gives consumption at time T if the state of the world is ω. The space of random variables representing state contingent consumption at time T is denoted by $\mathcal{X}$. For ease of exposition $\mathcal{X}$ is chosen to be the space of square integrable random variables, i.e.

$$\mathcal{X} = \{X \mid X \quad \mathcal{F}\text{-measurable, } E[X^2] < \infty\} \tag{3.1.1}$$

The following subsets of $\mathcal{X}$ will be of interest in what follows.

$$\mathcal{X}_+ := \{X \in \mathcal{X} \mid X \geq 0 \quad \text{a.s.}\}$$

$$\mathcal{X}_{++} := \{X \in \mathcal{X}_+ \mid E[X] > 0\}$$

Agents are characterized by their preferences on the space of consumption plans $\mathbb{R}_+ \times \mathcal{X}$, i.e. by complete, reflexive and transitive relations $\succsim$ on $\mathbb{R}_+ \times \mathcal{X}$. It is assumed that agents prefer more consumption to less. An agent will strictly prefer a consumption plan that differs from another by either a positive amount of time zero consumption or by a random variable that does not decrease time T consumption but will increase it with positive probability, i.e. agents' preferences are *strictly increasing* in the following sense.

For all $(c_o, X) \in \mathbb{R}_+ \times \mathcal{X}$, $c_o' \in \mathbb{R}_{++}$ and $X' \in \mathcal{X}_{++}$

$$\begin{aligned} (c_o + c_o', X) &\gg (c_o, X) \\ (c_o, X + X') &\gg (c_o, X) \end{aligned} \tag{3.1.2}$$

holds true.

Each agent has an initial endowment $e_a \in \mathbb{R}_{++}$.

There are (K+1) securities that allow for substitution of time zero consumption for time T consumption. The set of trading dates of these securities is given by [O,T]. The prices of securities are described by a (K+1)-dimensional stochastic process

$$S : [0,T] \times \Omega \to \mathbb{R}_+^{K+1}$$

with components $S^o, \ldots, S^K$. S^k, $k \in \{0, \ldots, K\}$, represents the prices of security k, i.e. $S_t^k(\omega)$ gives the price of security k at time t if the state of the world is ω. The information available is described by a *filtration* $\mathbb{F} := (\mathcal{F}_t)_{t \in [0,T]}$ on $(\Omega, \mathcal{F}, P)$, i.e. by an increasing family of σ-algebras. It is assumed that $\mathbb{F}$ fulfills the *usual conditions* as well as

$$\mathcal{F}_o = \mathcal{A}(\{F \in \mathcal{F} \mid P(F) = 0\}) \tag{3.1.3}$$

and

$$\mathcal{F}_T = \mathcal{F} . \tag{3.1.4}$$

All S^k, $k \in \{0,\dots,K\}$ are adapted to the information structure and have paths that are right continuous with left limits. For ease of exposition it is assumed that $S_T^k \in X$ for all $k \in \{1,\dots,K\}$. S^0 denotes a riskless security (bond) which is assumed to be of the form

$$S_t^0 = 1 \quad \forall t \in [0,T] \tag{3.1.5}$$

Thus a discounted model will be considered. (See Chapter 5 on the relaxation of (3.1.5).)

The following assumptions will be made throughout.

Securities do not yield dividends. (3.1.6)

There are no transaction costs in buying or selling of securities. (3.1.7a)

Unlimited short sales are feasible. (3.1.7b)

Securities are perfectly divisible. (3.1.7c)

The *continuous-time securities market model* consists of the probability space (Ω,F,P), the set $[0,T]$ of trading dates, the information structure $\mathbb{F}$ and the security price process S.

Now the decision problem of an agent at time zero concerning his consumption plan (c_0,X) is considered. The plan of an agent consists of a consumption plan and a trading strategy ϕ. A *trading strategy* is a $(K+1)$-dimensional stochastic process

$$\phi : [0,T] \times \Omega \to \mathbb{R}^{K+1}$$

with components $\phi^0,\dots,\phi^K$ that are assumed to be predictable. The assumption of predictability means that trading strategies depend only on past prices. In the case of continuous price movements this entails dependence on current prices as well, whereas in the case of price jumps this assumption means that agents cannot anticipate jumps. The real number $\phi_t^k(\omega)$ gives the number of units of security k in the portfolio of an agent at time t if the state of the world is ω. The value of a portfolio, which is held according to strategy ϕ is given by

$$(\phi_t\, S_t)(\omega) := \sum_{k=0}^{K} \phi_t^k(\omega)\, S_t^k(\omega)$$

at time t if the state of the world is ω. It will also be denoted by $V_t(\phi)(\omega)$ and $V(\phi)$ is called the *value process associated with* ϕ. To begin with special trading strategies will be considered.

3.1.1 Definition

A *simple trading strategy* ϕ is given by a finite set of trading dates

$$\{t_i \in [0,T] \mid i=0,\ldots,N,\ 0 = t_0 < t_1 < \ldots < t_N = T\} \tag{3.1.8}$$

and components of the form

$$\phi_t^k := \phi_{-1}^k\, 1_{\{0\}}(t) + \phi_0^k\, 1_{(0,t_1]}(t) + \ldots + \phi_{N-1}^k\, 1_{(t_{N-1},T]}(t)$$

$$k \in \{0,\ldots,K\}, \tag{3.1.9}$$

where ϕ_i^k is assumed to be F_{t_i} measurable for all $i \in \{0,\ldots,N-1\}$, $k \in \{0,\ldots,K\}$ and ϕ_{-1}^k is F_0-measurable for all $k \in \{0,\ldots,K\}$. All $|\phi_i^k|$, $i \in \{0,\ldots,N-1\}$, $k \in \{1,\ldots,K\}$, are bounded and ϕ_i^0, $i \in \{0,\ldots,N-1\}$ is square integrable.

Remark

ϕ of the form (3.1.8) and (3.1.9) is a leftcontinuous stochastic process with piecewise constant paths. The set (3.1.8) is called the *subdivision of* $[0,T]$ *associated with* ϕ (cf. DELLACHERIE/MEYER (1982), p. 312) and is denoted by $T(\phi)$. Note that in Definition 3.1.1 every finite subdivision of $[0,T]$ is a feasible set of trading dates. It is easily seen that ϕ^k, $k \in \{0,\ldots,K\}$ of the form (3.1.9) is predictable.

An agent employing a simple trading strategy ϕ faces the budget constraint

$$c_0 + V_0(\phi) \le e \quad {}^{1),2)}$$

1) Note that S is rightcontinuous by assumption.

2) The dependence on the agent will be suppressed.

at time zero and the budget constraints

$$\sum_{k=0}^{K} \phi_i^k \, S_{t_i}^k \le \sum_{k=0}^{K} \phi_{i-1}^k \, S_{t_i}^k \quad ^{1)} \qquad \text{a.s.}$$

at times t_i , $i \in \{0,\dots,N-1\}$. $\sum_{k=0}^{K} \phi_i^k \, S_{t_i}^k$ will be abbreviated in what follows by $\phi_i \, S_{t_i}$.

A consumption plan (c_o, X) is called *feasible* if there exists a simple trading strategy ϕ such that

$$c_o + V_o(\phi) \le e \tag{3.1.10}$$

$$\phi_i \, S_{t_i} \le \phi_{i-1} \, S_{t_i} \qquad \forall\, i \in \{0,\dots,N-1\} \text{ a.s.} \tag{3.1.11}$$

$$V_T(\phi) = X \quad P \text{ a.s.} \tag{3.1.12}$$

The set of feasible consumption plans is denoted by M_o .

$$M_o := \{(c_o, X) \in \mathbb{R}_+ \times X \mid \text{there exists a simple trading strategy with (3.1.10)-(3.1.12)}\}$$

The decision problem of an agent who is allowed to trade at only a finite number of otherwise arbitrary dates between zero and T can be formalized as follows. Find a consumption plan $(c_o^*, X^*) \in M_o$ such that

$$(c_o^*, X^*) \gtrsim (c_o, X) \qquad \forall\, (c_o, X) \in M_o \ . \tag{3.1.13}$$

Since by assumption agents' preferences are strictly increasing and $S^o \equiv 1$, only trading strategies with

$$c_o + V_o(\phi) = e \tag{3.1.14}$$

$$\phi_i \, S_{t_i} = \phi_{i-1} \, S_{t_i} \qquad \text{a.s.} \qquad \forall\, i \in \{0,\dots,N-1\} \tag{3.1.15}$$

will be considered. Trading strategies fulfilling (3.1.14) and (3.1.15) neither require nor generate funds between the initial and the final date. This gives rise to the following definitions.

---

1) Note that S is rightcontinuous by assumption.

3.1.2 Definition

A simple trading strategy ϕ is called *selffinancing* if (3.1.15) holds true. The set of simple selffinancing trading strategies is denoted by Φ_o.

The set of consumption plans that can be achieved by means of selffinancing trading strategies is denoted by M, i.e.

$$M := \{(c_o, X) \in \mathbb{R}_+ \times X \mid \text{there exists a simple trading strategy with (3.1.14), (3.1.15), (3.1.12)}\}$$

3.1.3 Definition

A contingent claim X is called *simply attainable*, if there exists a simple selffinancing trading strategy ϕ with (3.1.12). ϕ is also said to *generate the contingent claim in a selffinancing way*. The set of simply attainable contingent claims will be denoted by X_o.

3.2 Arbitrage and equivalent martingale measures

This section makes use of some of the concepts developed by HARRISON/KREPS (1979). Nevertheless, it should be emphasized that the set of trading strategies that agents may employ differ in fundamental ways from those given in HARRISON/KREPS (1979). (cf. p.57 below)

The basic assumption in ensuring the existence of a price system on the space of contingent claims that is consistent with the security price process S in a certain sense is the absence of arbitrage opportunities. It should not be possible to make a profit with positive probability and not facing the risk of a loss.

3.2.1 Definition

A simple selffinancing trading strategy ϕ is called a *simple arbitrage opportunity or simple free lunch* if $V_T(\phi) \in X_{++}$ with $V_o(\phi) = 0$ holds true.

The basic assumption that is made throughout is the following.

No arbitrage

There is no simple arbitrage opportunity. (3.2.1)

Assuming (3.2.1) the following lemma is obtained almost immediately.

3.2.2 Lemma

If (3.2.1) holds,

$$\pi(X) := V_0(\phi)$$

defines a strictly positive price system on X_0, i.e. π is linear, nonnegative on $X_0 \cap X_+$ and positive on $X_0 \cap X_{++}$.

Proof:

First of all, it is shown that π is well-defined. If $V_T(\phi) = V_T(\psi)$ P a.s. with $V_0(\phi) \neq V_0(\psi)$, without loss of generality consider the case $V_0(\phi) < V_0(\psi)$. A selffinancing trading strategy $\tilde{\phi}$ is defined by

$$\tilde{\phi}_t := (V_0(\psi) - V_0(\phi), 0, \ldots, 0) \qquad \forall\, t \in [0,T].$$

Then $\phi - \psi + \tilde{\phi}$ is a simple arbitrage opportunity. Now consider $V_T(\phi) \geq 0$ a.s. If $V_0(\phi) < 0$, $\psi := \phi - \tilde{\phi}$, where $\tilde{\phi}$ is defined by

$$\tilde{\phi}_t := (V_0(\phi), 0, \ldots, 0) \qquad \forall\, t \in [0,T],$$

would yield a simple arbitrage opportunity. □

One may ask whether there exists a "well-behaved" extension of π to all of X. It will be examined under what conditions there exists a continuous (in the L^2 norm on X) extension of π to X that is strictly positive on X_{++}. Such a price functional is called consistent with the given price process S.

3.2.3 Definition

A *consistent price system on the space of contingent claims* is a linear, continuous mapping π^* on X, which is nonnegative on X_+, strictly positive on X_{++} and is an extension of π given in Lemma 3.2.2, i.e.

$$\pi^* | X_o = \pi .$$

As in HARRISON/KREPS (1979) the existence of a consistent price system on X can be guaranteed, if there exists at least one agent that can achieve an optimal consumption plan. Before proceeding to this result some further assumptions on agents' preferences have to be introduced. Agents' preferences are assumed to fulfill the following conditions.

Convexity (3.2.2)

For all $(c_o, X) \in \mathbb{R}_+ \times X$, the set

$\{(c_o', X') \in \mathbb{R}_+ \times X \,|\, (c_o', X') \succsim (c_o, X)\}$

is convex.

Continuity (3.2.3)

For all $(c_o, X) \in \mathbb{R}_+ \times X$, the sets

$\{(c_o', X') \in \mathbb{R}_+ \times X \,|\, (c_o', X') \succsim (c_o, X)\}$

$\{(c_o', X') \in \mathbb{R}_+ \times X \,|\, (c_o, X) \succsim (c_o', X')\}$

are closed in the product topology on $\mathbb{R}_+ \times X$ based on the Euclidian norm topology on $\mathbb{R}_+$ and the L^2-norm topology on X.

In analogy to Theorems 1 and 2 of HARRISON/KREPS (1979), p. 386, p. 390, one can show the following result.

3.2.4 Theorem

If (3.2.1) holds, the following statements are equivalent.

(a) there exists a consistent price system ψ on X.

(b) there exists an agent that can achieve an optimal plan, i.e. there exists $\succsim_a$, $(c_o^*, X^*) \in \mathbb{R}_+ \times X_o$ with $c_o^* + \pi(X^*) \leq e_a$ and $(c_o^*, X^*) \succsim_a (c_o, X)$ for all $(c_o, X) \in \mathbb{R}_+ \times X_o$ with $c_o + \pi(X) \leq e_a$.

(c) there exists an equivalent martingale measure P^*, i.e. a probability measure P^* that is equivalent to P with

$$f := \frac{dP^*}{dP} \in L^2(\Omega, F, P)$$

such that S becomes a vector martingale with respect to P^*.

Proof:

The proof of HARRISON/KREPS (1979) can almost be taken over.[1) □

Remark

As a consequence of Theorem 3.2.4 consistent price systems on the space of contingent claims can be described by means of equivalent martingale measures. The correspondence between consistent price systems and equivalent martingale measures is given by

$$P^*(F) = \psi(1_F) \quad \text{and } \psi(X) = E^*[X].$$

In this monograph consistent price systems will be dealt with in terms of the corresponding martingale measures.

The set of equivalent martingale measures is denoted by $\mathbb{P}(S)$. Theorem 3.2.4 motivates the following definition.

---

1) In proving the martingale property of S^k the following simple self-financing trading strategy has to be used for $B \in F_t$

$$\phi_s^k(\omega) := \begin{cases} 1 & s \in (t,u],\ \omega \in B \\ 0 & \text{otherwise} \end{cases} \qquad k \in \{1,\ldots,K\}$$

$$\phi_s^o(\omega) := \begin{cases} -S_t^k(\omega) & s \in (t,u],\ \omega \in B \\ S_u^k(\omega) - S_t^k(\omega) & s \in (u,T],\ \omega \in B \\ 0 & \text{otherwise} \end{cases}$$

$$\phi_s^l(\omega) = 0 \qquad \forall\, l \notin \{0,k\}$$

3.2.5 Definition

A continuous-time securities market model is called *viable* if $\mathbb{P}(S) \neq \emptyset$ holds true.

In what follows, it is always assumed that the securities market model considered is viable.

3.3 Examples

In this section some security price processes will be introduced that give rise to a viable securities market model.

3.3.1 Geometric Brownian motion

Let $W = (W_t)_{t \in [0,T]}$ be a Brownian motion on a probability space $(\Omega, \mathcal{F}, P)$. $\mathbb{F} = (\mathcal{F}_t)_{t \in [0,T]}$ denotes the filtration generated by W that fulfills the usual conditions. For positive real numbers S_0^1 and σ a security price process S^1 is defined by

$$S_t^1 = S_0^1 \exp(\sigma W_t - \frac{\sigma^2}{2} t) \qquad (3.3.1)$$

The set of equivalent martingale measures is not empty. In particular, $P \in \mathbb{P}(S^1)$. Using the independence of the increments of Brownian motion the martingale property of S^1 with respect to $((\Omega, \mathcal{F}, P), \mathbb{F})$ follows with $s < t$ from

$$E[S_t^1 | \mathcal{F}_s] = S_s^1 \, E[\frac{S_t^1}{S_s^1} | \mathcal{F}_s]$$

$$= S_s^1 \exp(- \frac{\sigma^2}{2} (t-s)) E[\exp(\sigma(W_t - W_s)) | \mathcal{F}_s]$$

$$= S_s^1 \exp(-\frac{\sigma^2}{2}(t-s))E[\exp(\sigma(W_t - W_s))]$$

$$= S_s^1 \qquad P \text{ a.s.}$$

It has been used that

$$E[\exp Y] = \exp(a + \frac{\tau^2}{2}) \tag{3.3.2}$$

holds true for a normally distributed random variable with mean a and variance τ^2.

Quite often the specification (3.3.1) can be justified by the central limit theorem. COX/ROSS/RUBINSTEIN (1979) show that suitable price sequences associated with discrete-time security price processes converge in distribution to (3.3.1). The importance of the specification (3.3.1) rests on the property that $\mathbb{P}(S^1)$ consists of a single element (see Chapter 4 on this). The continuity of the process S^1 is of minor importance (see also the security price process (3.3.3) below).

3.3.2 A process with a random variance

The process to be considered rests on an example given by HARRISON/PLISKA (1981), pp. 252 . It is intended to model the following phenomenon. A security price process evolves like a geometric Brownian motion up to a date t_o, when an event occurs, which influences the parameters of the process. One might think, for example, of the outcome of an election. Depending on the event, the security price process evolves like a geometric Brownian motion with a changed parameter up to time $t = T$.

Consider a Brownian motion W and an independent random variable 1_A on a probability space (Ω,F,P^*) with $P^*(A) := \theta^*$, $\theta^* \in (0,1)$. Concerning the existence of such a space one should note that (Ω,F,P^*) could be chosen as

$$(\Omega_1 \times \Omega_2, G \otimes A, P \otimes \tilde{P}^*)$$

where (Ω_1, G, P) denotes the probability space associated with Brownian motion and $(\Omega_2, A, \tilde{P}^*)$ a probability space with $\Omega_2 = \{\omega_{21}, \omega_{22}\}$, $A = A(\{\omega_{21}\})$ and $\tilde{P}^*(\{\omega_{21}\}) = \theta^*$. The following filtration will be considered.

$$F_t := \begin{cases} G_t \otimes \{\emptyset, \Omega_2\} & t < t_o \\ G_t \otimes A & t \geq t_o . \end{cases}$$

$(G_t)_{t \in [0,T]}$ denotes the filtration corresponding to Brownian motion that fulfills the usual conditions. For constants $t_o \in (0,T)$, $S_o^1, \sigma_i \in \mathbb{R}_{++}$, $i=0,1,2$, $\sigma_1 \neq \sigma_2$, a security price process S^1 is defined by

$$S_t^1 = 1_{[0,t_o]} S_o^1 \exp(\sigma_o W_t - \frac{\sigma_o^2}{2} t) \tag{3.3.3}$$

$$+ 1_{(t_o,T]} S_o^1 \{1_A \exp(\sigma_o W_{t_o} - \frac{\sigma_o^2}{2} t_o + \sigma_1 (W_t - W_{t_o}) - \frac{\sigma_1^2}{2} (t - t_o))$$

$$+ 1_{A^c} \exp(\sigma_o W_{t_o} - \frac{\sigma_o^2}{2} t_o + \sigma_2 (W_t - W_{t_o}) - \frac{\sigma_2^2}{2} (t - t_o))\}$$

Using the exponential formula (see the Appendix) it can be shown that (3.3.3) corresponds to the variance process

$$\sigma(t,\omega) = 1_{[0,t_o]}(t)\sigma_o + 1_{(t_o,T]}(t)(\sigma_1 1_A(\omega) + \sigma_2 1_{A^c}(\omega))$$

in

$$S_t^1 = S_o^1 + \int_0^t S_s^1 \sigma_s \, dW_s \qquad \forall t \in [0,T]$$

Taking into account that 1_A and W are independent, the martingale property of S^1 with respect to $((\Omega, F, P^*), \mathbb{F})$ is obtained as in 3.3.1. Thus $P(S) \neq \emptyset$ follows.

3.3.3 Geometric Poisson process

Let $N = (N_t)_{t\in[0,T]}$ be a Poisson process with parameter λ on a probability space $(\Omega,\mathcal{F},P)$. $\mathbb{F} = (\mathcal{F}_t)_{t\in[0,T]}$ denotes the filtration generated by N that fulfills the usual conditions. A security price process S^1 is given by

$$S_t^1 = S_0^1 \exp(N_t - \lambda((\exp 1) - 1)t) \qquad (3.3.4)$$

where S_0^1 is a positive constant. Proceeding as in 3.3.1 one can show that S^1 is a martingale with respect to $((\Omega,\mathcal{F},P),\mathbb{F})$, i.e. $\mathbb{P}(S^1) \neq \emptyset$

4 The Continuous-time Trading Model

This chapter extends the model described in Chapter 3 to the continuous-time trading case. It aims at deriving valuations of contingent claims in a model, where agents may rearrange their portfolios at every time $t \in [0,T]$. For that purpose continuous-time selffinancing trading strategies are introduced in Section 4.1. Continuous-time selffinancing trading strategies allow for continuously rearranging the basic securities without requiring nor generating funds between the initial date zero and the final date T. A continuous-time selffinancing trading strategy is defined as the limit of a sequence of simple selffinancing trading strategies with respect to a certain norm introduced on the space of all continuous-time trading strategies. This norm takes into account both gains or losses due to price changes and funds to be invested (which might of course be negative thus representing withdrawals) that are associated with a trading strategy. Continuous-time selffinancing trading strategies are characterized and the properties of the space of all continuous-time selffinancing trading strategies are determined. Furthermore it is examined whether contingent claims that are generated by continuous-time selffinancing trading strategies can be approximated by simply attainable contingent claims. Section 4.2 characterizes contingent claims that are generated by continuous-time selffinancing trading strategies. The characterization rests essentially on the concept of a stable subspace. The stable subspace considered is the space of all stochastic integrals with respect to the given security price processes. Under suitable regularity conditions, it is shown that a contingent claim, which is generated by a continuous-time selffinancing trading strategy, can be valued independently of preferences by the initial investment associated with the selffinancing generating trading strategy. Section 4.3 considers specific security price processes. For those security price processes the classes of contingent claims that can be generated by continuous-time selffinancing trading strategies are determined and valuation formulas are obtained. Section 4.4 bridges the gap between the valuation method proposed in this monograph and the valuation method to be found in the literature based on difference-differential equations. Complete models are dealt with in Section 4.5. A model is called complete, if every contingent claim can be generated by a selffinancing trading strategy. Section 4.6 shows by means of counterexamples which assumptions are indispensable for the results obtained in Chapter 4.

4.1 Continuous-time self-financing trading strategies

This section introduces continuous-time selffinancing trading strategies. Defining a continuous-time selffinancing trading strategy as the limit of a sequence of simple selffinancing trading strategies would be a natural procedure to choose.[1] Thus the problem is reduced to finding a suitable convergence concept on the space of all continuous-time trading strategies. Since our main concern is the value process $V(\phi) = \phi S$ that a trading strategy yields, strategies will be evaluated by their value processes. A norm is defined that takes into account both the value process of a trading strategy and the funds to be invested, which might of course be negative thus representing withdrawals. Before the definition of the norm can be given, the basic assumptions have to be introduced and some fundamental lemmas have to be derived.

It will always be assumed that the securities market model considered is viable, i.e. $\mathbb{P}(S) \neq \emptyset$ holds true. An equivalent martingale measure $P^* \in \mathbb{P}(S)$ is chosen, which is held fixed from now on. For expository reason we do not give the most general set of assumptions in this section. As in HARRISON/KREPS (1979), p. 384, and already stated in Section 3.3.1 it is assumed that the price processes of the basic securities and all contingent claims X fulfill

$$S_T^k \in L^2(P) \ , \ k \in \{1,\ldots,K\}, \ X \in L^2(P) \ . \qquad (4.1.1)$$

Furthermore, for all contingent claims X

$$X \in L^2(P^*) \Leftrightarrow X \in L^2(P) \qquad (4.1.2)$$

Remark

Assumptions (4.1.1) and (4.1.2) are not essential. They only help to clarify the basic ideas by exploiting the structure of the Hilbert space $H^2(P^*)$ of square integrable martingales with respect to $((\Omega,F,P^*),\mathbb{F}))$ and thus avoiding a lot of technicalities. All statements can be generalized to integrable random variables. Usually (4.1.1) is

---

1) MERTON/SAMUELSON (1974), pp. 85, consider the transition from discrete-time to continuous-time trading strategies, when the basic security price process is continuous, i.e. the security price process allows only for continuous price movements.

given in actual valuation problems. (4.1.2) does not mean a serious restriction, since the transition from the given probability measure to an equivalent martingale measure might only result in a loss of square integrability. (4.1.2) is always true for equivalent probability measures with bounded Radon-Nikodym derivatives.

Furthermore, the following assumption is needed.

Strong orthogonality (4.1.3)

For all $i \neq j$, $i,j \in \{0,\dots,K\}$ the stochastic processes $(S^i - S^i_0)$ and $(S^j - S^j_0)$ are strongly orthogonal.

Remark

For $K = 1$, the case most often encountered in applications, the assumption of strong orthogonality does not mean any restriction at all, since $S^0 - S^0_0$ and $S^1 - S^1_0$ are always strongly orthogonal. Assumption (4.1.3) guarantees that the portfolio space is large enough to span all sources of uncertainty. In particular, the strong orthogonality assumption guarantees the closure of certain subspaces of $\mathcal{H}^2(P^*)$. Most processes used in the extant literature on contingent claim valuation satisfy this orthogonality condition. The most familiar example is a K-dimensional geometric Brownian motion with independent components. (4.1.3) cannot be dispensed with as can be seen from Example 4.6.3 in Section 4.6 below.

The following lemma gives a characterization of simple selffinancing trading strategies. This characterization proves to be most helpful in what follows.

4.1.1 Lemma

Let ϕ be a simple trading strategy with associated subdivision $\mathcal{T}(\phi) = \{t_i \mid i=0,\dots,N\}$. ϕ is selffinancing if and only if the value process $V(\phi)$ associated with ϕ has the following stochastic integral representation

$$V_t(\phi) = \int_0^t \phi \, dS \qquad \forall\, t \in [0,T]$$

<u>Proof</u>:

Let ϕ be selffinancing, i.e. $\phi_{i-1} S_{t_i} = \phi_i S_{t_i}$ holds true for all $i \in \{0,\dots,N-1\}$. For $t \in (t_j, t_{j+1}]$, $j \in \{0,\dots,N-1\}$, we obtain

$$\int_0^t \phi\, dS = \phi_{-1} S_0 + \sum_{i=1}^{N} \phi_{i-1} (S_{t_i \wedge t} - S_{t_{i-1} \wedge t})$$

$$= \phi_{-1} S_0 + \phi_j (S_t - S_{t_j}) + \sum_{i=1}^{j} \phi_{i-1} (S_{t_i} - S_{t_{i-1}})$$

$$= \phi_j S_t + \sum_{i=0}^{j} \phi_{i-1} S_{t_i} - \sum_{i=1}^{j+1} \phi_{i-1} S_{t_{i-1}}$$

$$= \phi_j S_t + \sum_{i=0}^{j} \phi_i S_{t_i} - \sum_{i=1}^{j+1} \phi_{i-1} S_{t_{i-1}}$$

$$= \phi_j S_t$$

$$= V_t(\phi)$$

which yields the stated stochastic integral representation. On the other hand, $V_t(\phi) = \int_0^t \phi\, dS \quad \forall\, t \in [0,T]$ implies

$$\phi_j S_{t_{j+1}} - \phi_{j-1} S_{t_j} = V_{t_{j+1}}(\phi) - V_{t_j}(\phi)$$

$$= \int_0^{t_{j+1}} \phi\, dS - \int_0^{t_j} \phi\, dS$$

$$= \phi_{-1} S_0 + \phi_j (S_{t_{j+1}} - S_{t_j}) + \sum_{i=1}^{j} \phi_{i-1} (S_{t_i} - S_{t_{i-1}})$$

$$- \phi_{-1} S_0 - \sum_{i=1}^{j} \phi_{i-1} (S_{t_i} - S_{t_{i-1}})$$

$$= \phi_j S_{t_{j+1}} - \phi_j S_{t_j}$$

for all $j \in \{0,\dots,N-1\}$, yielding the property of ϕ being selffinancing immediately. □

The interpretation of the integral representation of the value process associated with a simple selffinancing trading strategy is straightforward. For all $j \in \{0,\dots,N-1\}$ the stochastic integral $\int_0^{t_j} \phi\, dS$ is given by

$$\int_0^{t_j} \phi\, dS = \phi_{-1} S_0 + \int_0^{t_j} \phi\, d(S - S_0) = \phi_{-1} S_0 + \sum_{i=1}^{j} \phi_{i-1} (S_{t_i} - S_{t_{i-1}}) ,$$

which is the sum of the initial investment in the portfolio and the gains or losses resulting from changes in the prices of securities up to time t_j. Thus there are no other sources of gains or losses, which is obviously the same as being selffinancing.

The following lemma gives an important property of the value process associated with a simple selffinancing trading strategy.

4.1.2 Lemma

The value process associated with a simple selffinancing trading strategy is a square integrable martingale with respect to $((\Omega,\mathcal{F},P^*),\mathbb{F})$.

Proof:

Let ϕ be a simple selffinancing trading strategy with associated subdivision

$$\mathcal{T}(\phi) = \{t_i \mid i=0,\dots,N,\ 0 = t_0 < t_1 < \dots < t_N = T\}.$$

It is easily seen that $V_T(\phi)$ is square-integrable. Since ϕ has left-continuous paths and S is cadlag, $V(\phi)$ has paths with left limits. The right-continuity follows from ϕ being self-financing. The martingale property results as follows. Consider $s,t \in [0,T]$ with $s<t$. There exist j and l such that $t \in (t_j,t_{j+1}]$ and $s \in (t_l,t_{l+1}]$. The martingale property is obvious in the case $j=l$.

Using the standard properties of conditional expectation and (3.1.15) repeatedly, we get for $l < j$

$$\begin{aligned} E^*[V_t(\phi)|\mathcal{F}_s] &= E^*[\phi_j S_t|\mathcal{F}_s] \\ &= E^*[E^*[\phi_j S_t|\mathcal{F}_{t_j}]|\mathcal{F}_s] \\ &= E^*[\phi_j E^*[S_t|\mathcal{F}_{t_j}]|\mathcal{F}_s] \\ &= E^*[\phi_j S_{t_j}|\mathcal{F}_s] \\ &= E^*[\phi_{j-1} S_{t_j}|\mathcal{F}_s] \\ &= E^*[\phi_l S_{t_{l+1}}|\mathcal{F}_s] \\ &= \phi_l S_s \\ &= V_s(\phi) \qquad P^* \text{ a.s.} \quad \square \end{aligned}$$

Lemma 4.1.2 shows that the value process associated with a simple selffinancing trading strategy is an element of the Hilbert space $\mathcal{H}^2(P^*)$ of square integrable martingales with respect to P^*. Thus it seems plausible to use the norms available on $\mathcal{H}^2(P^*)$ in constructing a norm on the space of continuous-time trading strategies.

Consider a simple trading strategy which is not necessarily self-financing. The funds to be invested or to be withdrawn associated with ϕ are given by

$$C_t(\phi) := \sum_{i=0}^{j} (\phi_i - \phi_{i-1}) S_{t_i} \quad \text{if } t \in (t_j, t_{j+1}] \quad .$$

This yields the following decomposition of the value process associated with a simple trading strategy into initial investment, gains or losses due to changes in S and funds to be invested or to be withdrawn.

$$V_t(\phi) = \phi_{-1} S_0 + \sum_{i=1}^{N} \phi_{i-1} (S_{t_i \wedge t} - S_{t_{i-1} \wedge t}) + C_t(\phi) \tag{4.1.4}$$

(4.1.4) can also be represented by

$$V_t(\phi) = \int_0^t \phi dS + C_t(\phi) \quad . \tag{4.1.5}$$

Since $V(\phi)$ is the result of two effects, it is intuitively clear that at least two of the terms given in (4.1.5) have to be represented in the norm to be defined. We restrict the class of continuous-time trading strategies to include only strategies ϕ with $V(\phi)$ cadlag and

$$\| \phi \| := \| V(\phi) \|_m + (E^*[\int_0^T \phi_t^2 \, d[S,S]_t])^{1/2} < \infty \quad , \tag{4.1.6}$$

where $\| \cdot \|_m$ denotes the maximal norm and $[\ ,\ ]$ the optional quadratic variation (cf. the Appendix), i.e.

$$\| V(\phi) \|_m := (E^*[(\sup_{s \le T} |V_s(\phi)|)^2])^{1/2}$$

The resulting basic set of continuous-time trading strategies is denoted by Ψ_{P^*}

$$\Psi_{P^*} := \{\phi \mid \phi \text{ predictable, } V(\phi) \text{ cadlag, } \quad \| \phi \| < \infty\} \tag{4.1.7}$$

Identifying processes that are $\| \ \|$ indistinguishable and using the same notation for the resulting equivalence classes, we get

<u>4.1.3 Lemma</u>

$(\Psi_{P^*}, \| \ \|)$ is a normed space. $\| \ \|$ is equivalent to the norm $\| \ \|_*$ defined by

$$\| \phi \|_* := \| V(\phi) \|_m + \| \int \phi \, dS \|_m .$$

<u>Proof:</u>

If $\phi \in \Psi_{P^*}$, in particular $E^*[\int_0^T \phi^2 \, d[S,S]] < \infty$ holds true. Thus $(\int_0^t \phi \, dS)_{0 \le t \le T}$ defines an element of $H^2(P^*)$. The equivalence of the norms $\| \ \|$ and $\| \ \|_*$ follows from the property of isometry of the stochastic integral (cf. DELLACHERIE/MEYER (1982), p. 315) and the equivalence of the corresponding norms on $H^2(P^*)$. □

Having introduced the basic space $(\Psi_{P^*}, \| \cdot \|)$ of continuous-time trading strategies, continuous-time selffinancing trading strategies have to be defined. Selffinancing trading strategies will represent the means available to agents for transfering consumption between the initial date zero and the final date T. Because of Lemma 4.1.3 the following definition makes sense.

4.1.4 Definition

A trading strategy $\phi \in \Psi_{P^*}$ is called *selffinancing* if and only if there exists a sequence $(\phi_n)_{n \in \mathbb{N}}$, $\phi_n \in \Phi_o \ \forall n \in \mathbb{N}$, of simple selffinancing trading strategies such that

$$\| \phi - \phi_n \| \to 0$$

holds true. The set of all selffinancing trading strategies is denoted by Φ_{P^*}.

Since Definition 4.1.4 might not be that helpful in finding out whether a trading strategy is selffinancing indeed, the following theorem characterizes selffinancing trading strategies. Furthermore, properties of the space Φ_{P^*} of all selffinancing trading strategies are derived.

4.1.5 Theorem

(a) $\phi \in \Psi_{P^*}$ is selffinancing if and only if

$$V(\phi) = \int \phi \, dS$$

holds true.

(b) Define $\| \cdot \|_m$ and $\| \cdot \|_2$ on Ψ_{P^*} by

$$\| \phi \|_m := (E^*[(\sup_{t \le T} | V_t(\phi) |)^2])^{1/2}$$

$$\| \phi \|_2 := (E^*[(V_T(\phi))^2])^{1/2} .$$

$\| \ \|$, $\| \ \|_m$ and $\| \ \|_2$ are equivalent norms on Φ_{P^*}.

(c) $(\Phi_{P^*}, \| \ \|)$ is a complete normed space.

Proof:

(a) Consider $\phi \in \Phi_{P^*}$. By definition there exists a sequence $(\phi_n)_{n \in \mathbb{N}}$ of simple selffinancing trading strategies with $\|\phi_n - \phi\| \to 0$. In particular, by Lemma 4.1.3

$$V(\phi_n) \overset{H^2(P^*)}{\rightarrow} V(\phi)$$

and

$$\int \phi_n \, dS \overset{H^2(P^*)}{\rightarrow} \int \phi \, dS .$$

By Lemma 4.1.1 we get

$$V(\phi_n) = \int \phi_n \, dS$$

for all $n \in \mathbb{N}$. This implies

$$V(\phi) = \int \phi \, dS .$$

Consider ϕ with $V(\phi) = \int \phi \, dS$. For every $k \in \{1,\dots,K\}$ there exists a sequence $(\phi_n^k)_{n \in \mathbb{N}}$ of simple, uniformly bounded components of trading strategies with

$$\int \phi_n^k \, dS^k \overset{H^2(P^*)}{\rightarrow} \int \phi^k \, dS^k .$$

To see this, note that those integrands form a dense subset of the space of all integrands and that the stochastic integral defines an isometry. Thus we obtain

$$\sum_{k=1}^{K} \int \phi_n^k \, dS^k \overset{H^2(P^*)}{\rightarrow} \sum_{k=1}^{K} \int \phi^k \, dS^k .$$

Let $T(\phi_n) := \{0 = t_0 < t_1^n < \dots < t_{N_n}^n = T\}$ be the subdivision of $[0,T]$ that is associated with $\phi_n^1,\dots,\phi_n^K$. Choose ϕ_n^0 as follows

$$(\phi_n^0)_{-1} = \phi_0^0 \tag{4.1.8}$$

$$(\phi_n^o)_i = (\phi_n^o)_{i-1} + \sum_{k=1}^{K} (\phi_n^k)_{i-1} S_{t_i^n} - \sum_{k=1}^{K} (\phi_n^k)_i \, S_{t_i^n} \quad , \qquad (4.1.9)$$

$$i=0,\dots,N_n-1$$

(4.1.8) guarantees the convergence of $\int \phi^n \, dS$ to $\int \phi dS$ in $\mathcal{H}^2(P^*)$. (4.1.9) gives a selffinancing ϕ^n for every $n \in \mathbb{N}$. It follows that

$$\| \phi_n - \phi \| \to 0$$

holds true.

(b) This follows from (a) and the equivalence of the corresponding norms in $\mathcal{H}^2(P^*)$.

(c) Let $(\phi_n)_{n \in \mathbb{N}}$ be a Cauchy sequence in $(\Phi_{P^*}, \| \ \|)$. Then $(V(\phi_n))$ and $(\int \phi_n \, dS)$ are Cauchy sequences in $\mathcal{H}^2(P^*)$. Since $S - S_o$ has strongly orthogonal components, $(\int \phi_n^k \, d(S^k - S_o^k))$ is a Cauchy sequence for every $k \in \{1,\dots,K\}$. Since $\mathcal{H}^2(P^*)$ is complete and the stochastic integral defines an isometry, there exist predictable ϕ^k, $k \in \{1,\dots,K\}$ that fulfil the integrability condition necessary for the existence of the stochastic integral with

$$\int \phi_n^k \, d(S^k - S_o^k) \overset{\mathcal{H}^2(P^*)}{\to} \int \phi^k \, d\,(S^k - S_o^k)$$

and there exists $M \in \mathcal{H}^2(P^*)$ with

$$V(\phi_n) \overset{\mathcal{H}^2(P^*)}{\to} M \ .$$

Define ϕ^o by

$$\phi^o := M_o - \sum_{k=1}^{K} \phi_o^k \, S_o^k + \sum_{k=1}^{K} \left(\int \phi^k \, dS^k \right)_- - \sum_{k=1}^{K} \phi^k \, S_-^k \ .$$

This gives an element $\phi \in \Phi_{P^*}$ with $\| \phi^n - \phi \| \to 0$. Note that ϕ is self-financing by the standard properties of stochastic integrals.

Remark:

Obviously,

$$V_t(\phi) = \int_0^t \phi dS$$

is equivalent to

$$V_t(\phi) = V_0(\phi) + \int_0^t \phi\, d(S - S_0)$$

As in the case of a simple trading strategy the stochastic integral $\int \phi\, d(S - S_0)$ gives the gains or losses resulting from changes in the prices of securities. Theorem 4.1.5 shows that 4.1.4 is a reasonable definition. Φ_{P*} is the "natural" extension of the space of simple self-financing trading strategies. Moreover, every selffinancing trading strategy can be approximated by a simple selffinancing trading strategy either in mean square or in the maximal norm $\|\ \|_m$.

The following definition extends the notion of a simply attainable contingent claim to the space Φ_{P*} just introduced.

4.1.6 Definition

A contingent claim X is called *P*-attainable*, if and only if there exists a selffinancing trading strategy $\phi \in \Phi_{P*}$ such that (3.1.12) holds true. ϕ is also said to *generate the contingent claim in a selffinancing way*. The set of P*-attainable contingent claims will be denoted by X_{P*}.

Remark

Every simply attainable contingent claim is P*-attainable, since $\Phi_0 \subset \Phi_{P*}$.

The relationship between simple selffinancing trading strategies and elements of Φ_{P*} implies a similar one between simply attainable contingent claims and P*-attainable contingent claims, which is shown in the following theorem.

4.1.7 Theorem

A contingent claim X is P*-attainable if and only if there exists a sequence $(X_n)_{n \in \mathbb{N}}$ of simply attainable contingent claims such that X_n converges to X in mean square.

Proof:

Let X be P^*-attainable. We denote its generating selffinancing trading strategy by ϕ. Since $\phi \in \Phi_{P^*}$, by Definition 4.1.4 there exists a sequence $(\phi_n)_{n \in \mathbb{N}}$ of simple selffinancing trading strategies, the value processes $V(\phi_n)$ of which converge to $V(\phi)$ in $H^2(P^*)$ by Theorem 4.1.5. Define X_n by $X_n := V_T(\phi_n)$. Then X_n is simply attainable for every $n \in \mathbb{N}$. Since $\|\cdot\|_m$ and $\|\cdot\|_2$ are equivalent norms on $H^2(P^*)$, X_n converges to X in $L^2(P^*)$.

Now consider a sequence $(X_n)_{n \in \mathbb{N}}$ of simply attainable contingent claims that converges to a contingent claim X in mean square ($L^2(P^*)$). There exists a sequence $(\phi_n)_{n \in \mathbb{N}}$ of simple selffinancing trading strategies with $X_n = V_T(\phi_n)$ a.s. for every $n \in \mathbb{N}$. Theorem 4.1.5 implies that $(\phi_n)_{n \in \mathbb{N}}$ is a Cauchy sequence in $(\Phi_{P^*}, \| \ \|)$. By completeness it converges to a trading strategy $\phi \in \Phi_{P^*}$. With Theorem 4.1.5 we get $X = V_T(\phi)$ a.s. □

The following example gives an application of the results of this section.

4.1.8 Example

We consider a European call option on a stock with exercise price $K > 0$ and expiration date T. The value of this option at time T is given by $(S_T^1 - K)^+ := \max(0, S_T^1 - K)$, where S^1 denotes the price process of the basic stock. To see this, first consider the case $S_T^1 < K$. A rational investor will not exercise the option, since the price of the stock resulting from the option contract lies above the market price. Similarly, if $S_T^1 > K$ a rational investor will exercise the option. Since he or she will get the stock at a price K according to the option contract and will be able to sell it at the market price S_T^1, the value of the option is given as the difference between the stock price and the exercise price in this case. If the stock price at T equals the exercise price, it does not matter, whether or not the option is exercised. In both cases the value of the option is zero. Thus a European call option with exercise price K and expiration date

T gives rise to the contingent claim

$$X = (S_T^1 - K)^+ \tag{4.1.10}$$

at time T. The stock price process is assumed to be of the form (3.3.1). It will be examined whether the contingent claim X is P attainable for the martingale measure P given in 3.3.1. Thus the question is addressed, whether a European call option can be generated by a continuously adjusted portfolio in a riskless bond and the given stock in this model. The starting point is the following. Since a P-attainable contingent claim gives rise to a P-square integrable martingale, we try to determine a generating trading strategy $\phi \in \Phi_P$ from

$$\phi_t^o + \phi_t^1 S_t^1 = E[X|F_t] \tag{4.1.11}$$

First of all, the conditional expectation $E[X|F_t]$ will be determined. Using the Markov property[1] and the stochastic independence of the increments of Brownian motion we get

$$E[X|F_t] = E[(S_T^1 - K)^+|F_t]$$

$$= E[(S_T^1 - K)1_{\{S_T^1 > K\}} | F_t]$$

$$= E[S_T^1 1_{\{S_T^1 > K\}} |A(S_t^1)] - KE[1_{\{S_T^1 > K\}} |A(S_t^1)]$$

$$= S_t^1 E[\frac{S_T^1}{S_t^1} 1_{\{\frac{S_T^1}{S_t^1} > \frac{K}{S_t^1}\}} |A(S_t^1)] - KE[1_{\{\frac{S_T^1}{S_t^1} > \frac{K}{S_t^1}\}} |A(S_t^1)]$$

$$= S_t^1 \Phi\left(\frac{\ln S_t^1 - \ln K + \frac{\sigma^2}{2}(T-t)}{\sigma\sqrt{T-t}}\right) - K\Phi\left(\frac{\ln S_t^1 - \ln K - \frac{\sigma^2}{2}(T-t)}{\sigma\sqrt{T-t}}\right)$$

---

1) $f(S^1) := (S^1 - K)^+$ has the Markov property, since it is an increasing function of a process S^1 that has the Markov property (cf. GIHMAN/ SKOROHOD (1972), p. 64).

We used a result that reduces the calculation of conditional expectations to the calculation of ordinary expectations (cf. CHOW/TEICHER (1978), p. 201, Corollary 2) as well as

$$E[1_{\{\exp Y > K\}} \exp Y] = \exp(a + \frac{\tau^2}{2})\, \Phi\, (\frac{a + \tau^2 - \ln K}{\tau}) \tag{4.1.12}$$

$$P(\{\exp Y > K\}) = \Phi(\frac{a - \ln K}{\tau}) \tag{4.1.13}$$

for a normally distributed random variable Y with mean a and variance τ^2.

Thus

$$\phi_t^o = -K\, \Phi\, (\frac{\ln S_t^1 - \ln K - \frac{\sigma^2}{2}(T-t)}{\sigma\sqrt{T-t}}) \tag{4.1.14}$$

$$\phi_t^1 = \Phi\, (\frac{\ln S_t^1 - \ln K + \frac{\sigma^2}{2}(T-t)}{\sigma\sqrt{T-t}}) \tag{4.1.15}$$

is a solution of (4.1.11). ϕ^o and ϕ^1 are predictable. It remains to show that this trading strategy is selffinancing. In doing this the following notation will be used.

$$g(t,S^1) := \frac{\ln S^1 - \ln K + \frac{\sigma^2}{2}(T-t)}{\sigma\sqrt{T-t}}$$

$$h(t,S^1) := \frac{\ln S^1 - \ln K - \frac{\sigma^2}{2}(T-t)}{\sigma\sqrt{T-t}}$$

Note that

$$h(t,S^1) = g(t,S^1) - \sigma\sqrt{T-t}$$

holds true.

ϕ is a semimartingale[1)], thus one can apply Ito's lemma. Since ϕ as well as S^1 is continuous, we get

$$V_t(\phi) = \phi_t^o + \int_o^t \phi_-^1 \, dS^1 + \int_o^t S_-^1 \, d\phi^1 + [\phi^1, S^1]_t$$

It remains to show that

$$C_t := (\phi_t^o - \phi_o^o) + \int_o^t S^1 d(\phi^1 - \phi_o^1) + [\phi^1 - \phi_o^1, S^1]_t = 0$$

holds true for all $t \in [0,T]$. By Ito's lemma we get

$$\phi_t^o - \phi_o^o = -K\{\int_o^t (\frac{\partial\Phi(h)}{\partial s} + \frac{1}{2}\frac{\partial^2(\Phi(h))}{(\partial S^1)^2}\sigma^2(S^1)^2)ds + \int_o^t \frac{\partial\Phi(h)_-}{\partial S^1} dS^1\}$$

and

$$\phi_t^1 - \phi_o^1 = \int_o^t (\frac{\partial\Phi(g)}{\partial s} + \frac{1}{2}\frac{\partial^2(\Phi(g))}{(\partial S^1)^2}\sigma^2(S^1)^2)\,ds + \int_o^t \frac{\partial\Phi(g)_-}{\partial S^1} dS^1$$

The various terms will be determined in several steps. We will denote the density of Φ by n, i.e.

$$n(x) := \frac{1}{\sqrt{2\pi}} \exp\left(-\frac{1}{2}x^2\right)$$

and we will abbreviate $n(h(t,S^1))$ by $n(h)$ and $n(g(t,S^1))$ by $n(g)$. We get

(i) $$\frac{\partial\Phi(h)}{\partial t} = n(h)\frac{\partial h}{\partial t} = n(h)\frac{\frac{1}{2}\sigma^2\sqrt{T-t} + \frac{1}{2}(\ln\frac{S^1}{K} - \frac{1}{2}\sigma^2(T-t))(T-t)^{-1/2}}{\sigma\sqrt{T-t}}$$

$$= \frac{hn(h)}{2(T-t)} + \frac{\sigma n(h)}{2\sqrt{T-t}}$$

$$\frac{\partial\Phi(g)}{\partial t} = n(g)\frac{\partial g}{\partial t} = n(g)\left[\frac{\partial h}{\partial t} - \frac{\sigma}{2\sqrt{T-t}}\right] = \frac{hn(g)}{2(T-t)}$$

---

1) Since S^1 is a martingale, it trivially is a semimartingale. ϕ^o and ϕ^1 are semimartingales, since the semimartingale property is preserved under twice continuously differentiable functions (cf. ELLIOTT (1982), p. 140).

$$\text{(ii)}\quad \frac{\partial \Phi(h)}{\partial S^1} = n(h)\,\frac{\partial h}{\partial S^1} = \frac{n(h)}{S^1\sigma\sqrt{T-t}}$$

$$\frac{\partial \Phi(g)}{\partial S^1} = n(g)\,\frac{\partial g}{\partial S^1} = \frac{n(g)}{S^1\sigma\sqrt{T-t}}$$

$$\text{(iii)}\quad \frac{\partial^2\Phi(h)}{(\partial S^1)^2} = \frac{1}{\sigma\sqrt{T-t}}\left\{-\frac{n(h)}{(S^1)^2} - \frac{hn(h)}{S^1}\frac{\partial h}{\partial S^1}\right\}$$

$$= \frac{-n(h)}{(S^1)^2\sigma\sqrt{T-t}} - \frac{hn(h)}{(S^1)^2\sigma^2(T-t)}$$

$$\text{(iv)}\quad \frac{\partial^2\Phi(g)}{(\partial S^1)^2} = \frac{1}{\sigma\sqrt{T-t}}\left\{-\frac{n(g)}{(S^1)^2} - \frac{gn(g)}{S^1}\frac{\partial g}{\partial S^1}\right\}$$

$$= \frac{-n(g)}{(S^1)^2\sigma\sqrt{T-t}} - \frac{gn(g)}{(S^1)^2\sigma^2(T-t)}$$

which yields

$$\phi_t^o - \phi_o^o = \int_o^t -K\,\frac{n(h)-}{S^1\sigma\sqrt{T-t}}\,dS^1$$

and

$$\phi_t^1 - \phi_o^1 = \int_o^t \frac{n(g)-}{S^1\sigma\sqrt{T-t}}\,dS^1 - \int_o^t \frac{\sigma n(g)}{\sqrt{T-t}}\,dt$$

Using the relationship

$$Kn(h) = S^1 n(g) \tag{4.1.16}$$

the following holds true

$$C = (\phi^o - \phi_o^o) + \int S^1 d(\phi^1 - \phi_o^1) + [\phi^1 - \phi_o^1, S^1]$$

$$= -\int K \frac{n(h)-}{S^1\sigma\sqrt{T-t}}\, dS^1 + \int \frac{S^1 n(g)_-}{S^1\sigma\sqrt{T-t}}\, dS^1 - \int \frac{S^1\sigma n(g)}{\sqrt{T-t}}\, dt + [\phi^1 - \phi^1_o, S^1]$$

$$= -\int \frac{S^1\sigma n(g)}{\sqrt{T-t}}\, dt + \int \frac{n(g)}{\sigma\sqrt{T-t}}\, d[\sigma W - \sigma^2 t, S^1]$$

$$= -\int \frac{S^1\sigma n(g)}{\sqrt{T-t}}\, dt + \int \frac{\sigma n(g)}{\sqrt{T-t}}\, d[W, \frac{S^1}{\sigma}]$$

$$= -\int \frac{S^1\sigma n(g)}{\sqrt{T-t}}\, dt + \int \frac{S^1\sigma n(g)}{\sqrt{T-t}}\, dt$$

In the last row a result on locally bounded integrands has been used (cf. DELLACHERIE/MEYER (1982), Theorem 22, p. 329). S^1 is locally bounded as a predictable cadlag process. Thus we get

$$\phi^o + \phi^1 S^1 = \int \phi^o\, dS^o + \int \phi^1\, dS^1$$

$$= \phi^o_o + \int \phi^1\, dS^1$$

i.e. ϕ is selffinancing.

Now a sequence of simple selffinancing trading strategies will be determined that approximates ϕ. Let

$$\mathcal{T}_n := \{t^n_i \in [0,T] \,|\, i=0,\dots,N,\; 0 = t^n_o < t^n_1 < \dots < t^n_N = T\}$$

be an equidistant subdivision of $[0,T]$ with $t^n_i - t^n_{i-1} = \frac{1}{n}$.
Define

$$(\phi^1_n)_{-1} := \phi^1_o = \Phi(g(0, S^1_o))$$

$$(\phi^1_n)_i := \phi^1_{t_i} = \Phi(g(t_i, S^1_{t_i}))$$

and $(\phi_n^o)_i$ as in (4.1.8), (4.1.9). Then we have

$$\int \phi_n \, dS \quad \overset{H^2(P^*)}{\rightarrow} \quad \int \phi \, dS$$

One concludes as in DELLACHERIE/MEYER (1982), p. 316. ϕ_n and ϕ are bounded by 1 and we have $\phi_n \rightarrow \phi$ pointwise. Moreover

$$E[(\int_o^T (\phi_n-\phi)dS)^2] = E[\ [\ \int(\phi_n-\phi)dS,\ \int(\phi_n-\phi)dS\ ]_T\ ]$$

$$= E[\int_o^T (\phi_n-\phi)^2 \, d[S,S]\ ]$$

By Lebesgue's theorem the right hand side converges to zero. Thus the assertion follows from Lemma 4.1.3 and Theorem 4.1.5.

Remarks

1. HARRISON/PLISKA (1981), pp. 232, 239, call a continuous-time trading strategy selffinancing if the associated portfolio value process fulfills

$$V_t(\phi) = V_o(\phi) + \int_o^t \phi \, dS$$

for all $t \in [O,T]$. This integral representation is correct only in the case $S_o^k = 0 \quad \forall\, k \in \{0,\ldots,K\}$. But this case is explicitly excluded in HARRISON/PLISKA (1981). Furthermore, no explanation as to the definition of a selffinancing trading strategy by the integral representation above is given. MERTON (1971), p. 379, MERTON (1973), p. 164, and MERTON/SAMUELSON (1974), pp. 85, also define a selffinancing trading strategy by means of an integral representation. This definition is motivated by the transition from a discrete-time to a continuous-time trading strategy in the case of a continuous security price process.

2. One might ask whether the given class of selffinancing trading strategies can be enlarged by replacing the deterministic trading dates t_i in (3.1.9) by stopping times.The following argument shows that

this is not the case. Consider stopping times

$T_o, \dots, T_{N-1}$ with

$$0 = T_o \le T_1 \le \dots \le T_{N-1} \le T \qquad (4.1.17)$$

and a trading strategy ϕ with components of the form

$$\phi_t^k := \phi_{-1}^k 1_{\{0\}}(t) + \phi_o^k 1_{]T_o,T_1]}(t) + \dots + \phi_{N-1}^k 1_{]T_{N-1},T]}(t) \qquad (4.1.18)$$

In (4.1.18) ϕ_i^k is assumed to be F_{t_i}-measurable for all $i \in \{0,\dots,N-1\}$, $k \in \{0,\dots,K\}$ and ϕ_{-1}^k is F_o-measurable for all $k \in \{0,\dots,K\}$. All $|\phi_i^k|$, $k \in \{1,\dots,K\}, i \in \{0,\dots,N-1\}$ are bounded. Since the σ-algebra of predictable sets is generated by the family of stochastic intervals of the form $]T_i,T_j]$ and $\{0\} \times F$, $F \in F_o$ (cf. MÉTIVIER (1982), Proposition 4.6, p. 13) it is obvious that ϕ of the form (4.1.17) and (4.1.18) is predictable. A strategy of this kind is called an *almost simple* trading strategy. The definition of a selffinancing trading strategy extends easily to almost simple trading strategies and the theory developped in this chapter applies equally to stopping times.

3. In Example 4.1.8 an approximating sequence of simple selffinancing trading strategies is given for the trading strategy that generates the contingent claim $(S_T^1 - K)^+$ associated with a European call option. Approximations of this kind are of interest in empirical studies. Up to now only simple trading strategies, which are not selffinancing, have been used for approximation purposes (cf. BHATTACHARYA (1980), p. 1082). The theory developed above shows that in general continuous-time self-financing trading strategies can be approximated by simple self-financing trading strategies. In particular, this is of interest for the purpose of hedging. The impossibility of continuous-time trading requires approximations to the theoretically found generating self-financing trading strategies in order to use them for actual hedging purposes. It is an important feature of the model considered that approximating trading strategies can be chosen such that they do not require any infusion of funds when rearranging the given securities.

4. HARRISON/KREPS(1979),pp. 399, discuss the problem whether free lunches appear if a class of trading strategies is allowed for that is larger than the class of simple selffinancing trading strategies. This is not the case with the class Φ_{P*} of selffinancing trading strategies introduced in this section. A *continuous-time arbitrage opportunity* or *free lunch* ϕ is defined in analogy to Definition 3.2.1, i.e. ϕ is an element of Φ_{P*} such that $V_0(\phi) = 0$ and $V_T(\phi) \in X_{++}$ holds true. Since the value process of any element of Φ_{P*} is a martingale with respect to P*, continuous-time free lunches do not exist within the class Φ_{P*} of selffinancing trading strategies.

4.2 A characterization of P*- attainable contingent claims

In Section 4.1 continuous-time selffinancing trading strategies are defined in dependence of a fixed given equivalent martingale measure P*. This dependence carries over to contingent claims that are generated by selffinancing trading strategies. This section shows that this dependence does not cause serious problems, since under suitable regularity conditions every P*- attainable contingent claim is also $\tilde{P}^*$-attainable for all $\tilde{P}^* \in \mathbb{P}(S)$. More than that, the valuation of a P*-attainable contingent claim by means of the initial investment associated with the generating selffinancing trading strategy is independent of the equivalent martingale measure chosen. Thus this valuation by means of initial investments can be interpreted as a preference independent or risk neutral valuation of contingent claims. These results are derived from a characterization of P*- attainable contingent claims.

One might expect that P*- attainable contingent claims can be characterized in exploiting the stochastic integral representation of the value processes associated with the generating selffinancing trading strategies.In fact,this is the case,as will be shown in Theorem 4.2.4 below. In order to get this characterization of P*- attainable contingent claims some concepts associated with stochastic integration have to be introduced. These concepts are discussed in detail because of their importance for the derivation to follow.

Let ϕ^k be a predictable process with

$$E^*[\int_0^T (\phi^k)^2 \, d[S^k,S^k]] < \infty .$$

Then the stochastic integral $\int \phi^k dS^k$ is defined, and it is a square integrable martingale with respect to $((\Omega,F,P^*),\mathbb{F})$, i.e.

$$\int \phi^k dS^k \in H^2(P^*).$$

Because of the linearity property of the stochastic integral, i.e.

$$\int (\lambda\phi^k + \mu\psi^k)dS^k = \lambda\int\phi^k dS^k + \mu\int\psi^k dS^k$$

for all $\lambda,\mu \in \mathbb{R}$ and predictable ϕ^k, ψ^k satisfying the integrability condition given above, we can speak of subspaces of $H^2(P^*)$ being generated by stochastic integrals. In what follows we will consider the subspace of $H^2(P^*)$, which is generated by stochastic integrals of the form $\int\phi^k dS^k$, $k \in \{0,\dots,K\}$, and we denote this subspace by $L_{P*}(S^0,\dots,S^K)$

$$L_{P*}(S^0,\dots,S^K) := \{c + \sum_{k=1}^{K} \int\phi^k dS^k \ , \ c \in \mathbb{R}, \ \phi^k \text{ predictable},$$

$$E^*[\int_0^T (\phi^k)^2 \, d[S^k,S^k]] < \infty \ , \ k \in \{1,\dots,K\}\} \tag{4.2.1}$$ 1)

It is easily seen that

$$L_{P*}(S^0,\dots,S^K) = L_{P*}(S^0,S^1-S_0^1,\dots,S^K-S_0^K) \tag{4.2.2}$$

holds true. Elements of $L_{P*}(S^0,\dots,S^K)$ are denoted by $\int\phi dS$.

$L_{P^*}(S^0,\dots,S^K)$ will often be abbreviated by $L(P^*)$ $(L(S^0,\dots,S^K))$, if it is obvious which process (equivalent martingale measure) is considered. For $(N^n)_{n \in \mathbb{N}}$, $N^n \in H^2(P^*)$, we consider the closure in $H^2(P^*)$ of the vec-

---

1) If $S_0^k > 0$ holds true for at least one $k > 0$, $L_{P*}(S^0,\dots,S^K)$ equals

$$L_{P*}(S^1,\dots,S^K) = \{\sum_{k=1}^{K} \int\phi^k dS^k, \ \phi^k \text{ predictable},$$

$$E^*[\int_0^T (\phi^k)^2 \, d[S^k,S^k]] < \infty \ , \ k \in \{1,\dots,K\}\}$$

since all $c \in \mathbb{R}$ can be obtained as stochastic integrals with respect to the given S^k with $S_0^k > 0$.

tor space $\bigcup_{n\in\mathbb{N}} L_{P*}(N^1,\dots,N^n)$, which will be denoted by $L_{P*}(\{N^n | n \in \mathbb{N}\})$.

The properties of $L(P*)$ are collected in the following lemma (cf. ELLIOTT(1982), pp 109,88).

4.2.1 Lemma

(a) $L(P*)$ is a closed subspace of $H^2(P*)$.
(b) $L(P*)$ is *closed with respect to stopping times*, i.e. for every stopping time τ and every $M \in L(P*)$, the process $M^\tau := (M_{t\wedge\tau})_{t\in[0,T]}$ is an element of $L(P*)$.
(c) For every $M \in L(P*)$ and $A \in F_0$, $1_A M \in L(P*)$ holds true.

Remark

A subspace of $H^2(P*)$ with the properties (a) - (c) is called a *stable subspace* of $H^2(P*)$.(cf. the Appendix).

Proof

We only show that $L(P*)$ is closed. Proofs of the other statements may be found for example, in ELLIOTT(1982).

Note that every

$$L_{P*}(S^k-S_0^k) := \{\int\phi^k d(S^k-S_0^k) \mid \phi^k \text{ predictable, } E^*[\int_0^T(\phi^k)^2 d[S^k,S^k]]<\infty\}$$

is a closed subspace of $H^2(P*)$ (cf. ELLIOTT(1982),p. 109). The strong orthogonality of the processes $S^k-S_0^k$, $k\in\{1,\dots,K\}$, implies the orthogonality in the Hilbert space sense of associated stochastic integrals (cf. the Appendix), i.e.

$$\sum_{k=1}^K E^*[(\int_0^T \phi^k\, d(S^k - S_0^k))^2]=E^*[(\sum_{k=1}^K \int_0^T \phi^k\, d(S^k - S_0^k))^2]$$

Thus $L(P*)$ is closed. □

In what follows we will consider the set of square integrable martingales that are orthogonal in the Hilbert space sense to the space $L(P*)$ and we will denote it by $(L(P*))^\perp$.

$$(L(P*))^\perp := \{M \in H^2(P*) \mid E^*[M_T L_T] = 0 \quad \forall\, L \in L(P*)\} \tag{4.2.3}$$

The properties of $(L(P^*))^\perp$ as given in ELLIOTT(1982) and DELLACHERIE/MEYER(1982) are reported in the following lemma, the proof of which is suppressed (cf. ELLIOTT(1982),pp. 88,DELLACHERIE/MEYER(1982),pp. 358)

4.2.2 Lemma

(a) $(L(P^*))^\perp$ is a closed subspace of $H^2(P^*)$.

(b) $(L(P^*))^\perp$ is closed with respect to stopping times.

(c) For every $M \in (L(P^*))^\perp$ and $A \in F_0$, $1_A M \in (L(P^*))^\perp$ holds true.

(d) If $L \in L(P^*)$ and $M \in (L(P^*))^\perp$, M and L are strongly orthogonal.

(e) $(L(P^*))^\perp = \{N \in H^2(P^*) \mid N$ is strongly orthogonal to every $L \in L(P^*)\}$

(f) $((L(P^*))^\perp)^\perp = L(P^*)$

Remark

Because of (e) $(L(P^*))^\perp$ also is called the *(strongly) orthogonal complement of* $L(P^*)$.

The following lemma examines the relationship between P^*-attainable contingent claims and elements of $L(P^*)$.(see also HARRISON/PLISKA (1981), Proposition 3.32)

4.2.3 Lemma

A contingent claim X is P*- attainable if and only if the square integrable martingale $(X_t)_{t\in[0,T]}$ defined by $X_t := E^*[X|F_t]$ is an element of $L(P^*)$.

Proof

If X is a P*- attainable contingent claim, we get $(X_t) \in L(P^*)$ by Theorem 4.1.5(a). Now consider $(X_t) \in L(P^*)$. There exist predictable processes ϕ^k with

$$E^*[\int_0^T (\phi_s^k)^2 \, d[S^k,S^k]_s] < \infty \ , \ k \in \{1,\ldots,K\}$$

and $c \in \mathbb{R}$ such that

$$X = c + \sum_{k=1}^{K} \int_0^T \phi^k \, dS^k \qquad P^* \text{ a.s.}$$

holds true. Define ϕ^0 by

$$\phi^0 := c + \sum_{k=1}^{K} (\int \phi^k \, dS^k)_- - \sum_{k=1}^{K} \phi^k S^k_- .$$

The standard properties of the stochastic integral and Theorem 4.1.5 imply that ϕ is self-financing and that it generates X. □

Before we can give the final characterization of P*- attainable contingent claims, the concept of an equivalent martingale measure has to be extended. A *P-continuous signed martingale measure* Q is defined by the following three properties:

(i) Q is a *signed measure* with $Q(\Omega) = 1$, i.e. Q is a σ-additive set function from $\mathcal{F}$ into $\mathbb{R}$ with $Q(\emptyset) = 0$ and $Q(\Omega) = 1$. (cf. HALMOS(1950),pp. 118)

(ii) Q is *P-continuous*, i.e. $Q(F) = 0$ for every $F \in \mathcal{F}$ for which $P(F) = 0$ holds true. Furthermore, the Radon-Nikodym derivative of Q with respect to P [1], which is denoted by M_T, is square integrable.

(iii) S is a *vector martingale with respect to* Q. i.e. if (M_t) is defined by $M_t := E[M_T|\mathcal{F}_t]$, $M\,S^k$ is a martingale with respect to $((\Omega,\mathcal{F},P),\mathbb{F})$ for all $k \in \{1,...,K\}$.

The set of all P-continuous signed martingale measures will be denoted by $\mathbb{Q}(S)$.

Remark

Because of (4.1.2) every element of $\mathbb{Q}(S)$ is a P*- continuous signed martingale measure with respect to S and every P*- continuous signed martingale measure with respect to S is an element of $\mathbb{Q}(S)$. The set of all equivalent martingale measures with respect to S is a subset of $\mathbb{Q}(S)$.

With the concepts introduced so far we can give the following characterization of P*- attainable contingent claims, which proves to be most helpful in actually determining the class of P*- attainable con-

---

1) See HALMOS(1950),p. 128, Theorem B, for the existence of the Radon-Nikodym derivative of Q with respect to P.

tingent claims for specific security price processes (cf. Section 4.3 below).

4.2.4 Theorem

A contingent claim X is P^*-attainable if and only if its expected value with respect to every P-continuous signed martingale measure is constant, i.e.

$$E^Q[X] = \text{constant} \qquad \forall\, Q \in \mathbb{Q}(S).$$

Proof

Let X be P^*-attainable. By Lemma 4.2.3 we get $(X_t) \in \mathcal{L}(P^*)$. Consider $Q \in \mathbb{Q}(S)$ and denote by M_T the Radon-Nikodym derivative of Q with respect to P^*. Let M be the P^*-martingale, which is defined by $M_t := E^*[M_T | \mathcal{F}_t]$ and N the P^*-martingale $N := M - 1$.

$$N\, S^k = (M - 1)\, S^k = M\, S^k - S^k$$

is a P^*-martingale, since it is the difference of the martingales MS^k and S^k. By $Q(\Omega) = 1$, we get $N_0 = M_0 - 1 = 0$. N is strongly orthogonal to $S^0, (S^1-S^1_0), \dots, (S^K-S^K_0)$. Since the strong orthogonality of N to S^0, $(S^1-S^1_0), \dots, (S^K-S^K_0)$ extends to stochastic integrals with respect to $(S^k-S^k_0)$, $k \in \{1,\dots,K\}$, (cf. JACOD (1979), p. 116, Theorème (4.7)), N is an element of $(\mathcal{L}(P^*))^\perp$. We get

$$E^Q[X] = E^*[M_T X] = E^*[N_T X] + E^*[X] = E^*[X].$$

Let $E^Q[X]$ be constant for all $Q \in \mathbb{Q}(S)$. Consider any $N \in (\mathcal{L}(P^*))^\perp$. It will be shown that $E^*[N_T X] = 0$ holds true. In order to do this, a martingale M is defined by $M := N + 1$. M_T is the Radon-Nikodym derivative of an element $Q^M \in \mathbb{Q}(S)$ defined by

$$Q^M(F) := \int_F M_T \, dP^* \qquad \forall\, F \in \mathcal{F}.$$

This follows, since $N \in (\mathcal{L}(P^*))^\perp$ and $P^* \in \mathbb{P}(S)$ imply that

$$M\, S^k = N\, S^k + S^k$$

is a martingale with respect to P^*. Furthermore, for any $N \in (\mathcal{L}(P^*))^\perp$

necessarily $N_o = 0$ holds true, which yields

$$Q^M(\Omega) = E^*[M_T] = E^*[N_T + 1] = N_o + 1 = 1.$$

Because of $P^* \in \mathbb{Q}(S)$, we obtain

$$E^*[X] = E^{Q^M}[X] = E^*[M_T X] = E^*[N_T X] + E^*[X],$$

i.e. $E^*[N_T X] = 0$. Since

$$E^*[N_T X] = 0 \qquad \forall\, N \in (L(P^*))^{\perp}$$

holds true, $(X_t) \in ((L(P^*))^{\perp})^{\perp}$.

By Lemma 4.2.2 (f) and Lemma 4.2.3 X is P^*-attainable. □

The following corollaries answer the question to which extent the dependence on the given equivalent martingale measure can be ignored.

4.2.5 Corollary

Suppose two equivalent martingale measures $P_1, P_2 \in \mathbb{P}(S)$ both satisfy the assumption (4.1.2). A contingent claim X is P_1^*-attainable if and only if it is P_2^*-attainable. In that case the initial investments associated with the generating selffinancing trading strategies coincide and equal $E^*[X]$.

Proof

If P_1 and P_2 both satisfy (4.1.2), $\mathbb{Q}(S)$ equals the set of P_1^*-continuous signed martingale measures as well as the set of P_2^*-continuous signed martingale measures. Now consider a P_1^*-attainable contingent claim which is also P_2^*-attainable. There exist $\phi \in \Phi_{P_1^*}$ and $\psi \in \Phi_{P_2^*}$ such that

$$X = V_T(\phi) = \int_0^T \phi\, dS$$

and

$$X = V_T(\psi) = \int_0^T \psi\, dS$$

holds true. This implies

$$\phi_o S_o = E^{P_1^*}[X] = E^{P_2^*}[X] = \psi_o S_o$$

and because of $P^* \in \mathbb{P}(S)$ this results in

$$\phi_o S_o = E^{P_1^*}[X] = E^*[X]. \qquad \square$$

An important special case of Corollary 4.2.5 arises, if the Radon-Nikodym derivatives of the elements of $\mathbb{P}(S)$ with respect to P^* are bounded a.s.

4.2.6 Corollary

If the Radon-Nikodym derivatives of all elements of $\mathbb{P}(S)$ with respect to P^* are bounded a.s., every P^*-attainable contingent claim is $\tilde{P}^*$-attainable for all equivalent martingale measures $\tilde{P}^* \in \mathbb{P}(S)$. The initial investments associated with the generating selffinancing trading strategies coincide and equal $E^*[X]$.

Corollaries 4.2.5 and 4.2.6 show that under certain regularity conditions the property of attainability is invariant under changes of equivalent martingale measures. This result can be shown to hold true without the conditions stated, if one extends the class of admissible trading strategies to the class of locally bounded trading strategies and employs semimartingale techniques.

What is the economic meaning of this result? Theorem 3.2.4 and in particular its proof (cf. HARRISON/KREPS (1979), pp. 386) show that the set of equivalent martingale measures can be interpreted as a set of different subjective probability measures that agents of the class considered may have. Corollary 4.2.6 states that for every P^*-attainable contingent claim there is a price that is independent of agents' subjective expectations formed according to equivalent martingale measures. All agents agree on the valuation $E^*[X]$ of a P^*-attainable contingent claim, even though they might have heterogeneous probability assessments. This heterogeneity shows up in the portfolio that an agent with a certain subjective probability measure out of the class of equivalent martingale measures will hold in order to generate X. To see this consider two agents with different subjective probability distributions $P_1, P_2 \in \mathbb{P}(S)$ and a contingent claim that is attainable under both equivalent martingale measures. There exist $\phi \in \Phi_{P_1^*}$ and $\psi \in \Phi_{P_2^*}$ such that

$$X = V_T(\phi) = V_T(\psi) \qquad P^* \text{ a.s.}$$

and

$$E^*[X] = V_o(\phi) = V_o(\psi) ,$$

whereas

$$V_t(\phi) = E^{P_1}[X|F_t], \quad \forall t \in [0,T]$$

and

$$V_t(\psi) = E^{P_2}[X|F_t] \quad \forall t \in [0,T] ,$$

which differ in general. Thus $E^*[X]$ can be interpreted as a preference free or risk neutral valuation of the contingent claim X. In the "agents' subjective probability measure" interpretation equivalent martingale measures with a.s. bounded Radon-Nikodym derivatives correspond to agents the probability assessments of which are subject to certain bounds with respect to each other.

The characterization of P^*-attainable contingent claims of Theorem 4.2.4 resembles the characterization that HARRISON/KREPS (1979), pp. 387, 392, give of contingent claims that *can be priced by arbitrage*. Even though HARRISON/KREPS (1979) use a different set of trading strategies, we may discuss their arbitrage pricing concept within the framework outlined in Chapter 3. HARRISON/KREPS (1979) consider contingent claim valuation in a multiperiod securities market model, where trading in the basic securities is only possible at a finite number of prespecified trading dates. Thus they only allow for special simple trading strategies. A simple selffinancing trading strategy is defined in analogy to (3.1.15) as in the discrete-time case. The difference between the basic set of simple trading strategies introduced in Section 3 and the set of simple trading strategies employed by HARRISON/KREPS (1979) lies in the fact that the latter consists of trading strategies that may depend on past and present prices of securities. Despite the different informational restrictions on agents' trading strategies, the concepts introduced in Section 3 make sense in both cases and the results given there apply to both sets of trading strategies. Thus we may speak of a viable securities market model in both cases. In the case of a viable securities market model, HARRISON/KREPS call a *price p for a contingent claim* X *consistent with* (X_o,π) if and only if the so defined augmented price system is viable. A *contingent claim* X is said to be *priced by arbitrage* if and only if there is a unique price for X that is consistent with (X_o,π). If this is the case, the unique consistent price is called the *arbitrage value* of the contingent claim X. HARRISON/KREPS show that a contingent claim can be priced by arbitrage if and only if it has the same value under every consistent price system.

Obviously, we have

4.2.7 Corollary

A P^*-attainable contingent claim X has the same price under every consistent price system. This price is given by $E^*[X]$.

Thus every P^*-attainable contingent claim X is priced by arbitrage and has the arbitrage value $E^*[X]$ as defined by HARRISON/KREPS (1979). The following theorem considers the question, whether the converse is also true. It gives sufficient conditions that guarantee the equivalence of P^*-attainability and arbitrage pricing in the sense of HARRISON/KREPS (1979). Thus given those conditions, the arbitrage value of a contingent claim is nothing else than the initial investment in a self-financing generating portfolio in the continuous-time trading model.

4.2.8 Theorem

Consider a securities market model that fulfills *at least one* of the following two assumptions:

Every element of

$$\mathcal{N} := \{N \mid N := M-1,\ M := (E^*[M_T \mid \mathcal{F}_t])_{t \in [0,T]}\ , \tag{4.2.4}$$

$$M_T := \frac{dQ}{dP^*}\ ,\ Q \in \mathbb{Q}(S)\ \}$$

is bounded.

$$\mathcal{N} = \mathcal{L}(\{N^n \mid n \in \mathbb{N}\})\ , \tag{4.2.5}$$

where all N^n are strongly orthogonal pairwise and are bounded.

Then a contingent claim is P^*-attainable if and only if it is priced by arbitrage in the sense of HARRISON/KREPS (1979).

Proof:

Because of Lemma 4.2.7 and the correspondence between consistent price systems and equivalent martingale measures given above (cf. Section 3.2), we only have to show that

$$E^Q[X] = \text{constant} \quad \text{for all } Q \in \mathbb{Q}(S)$$

is implied by

$$E^{\tilde{P}}[X] = \text{constant} \quad \text{for all } \tilde{P} \in \mathbb{P}(S)\ .$$

Consider $Q \in \mathbb{Q}(S)$, $Q \neq P^*$.

(i) Suppose (4.2.4) holds true. Let M_T denote the Radon-Nikodym derivative of Q with respect to P^*, M the P^*-martingale $(E^*[M_T \mid \mathcal{F}_t])_{t \in [0,T]}$ and N the P^*-martingale N := M-1. N is an element of $(\mathcal{L}(P^*))^{\perp}$ and it is bounded by assumption. Define a P^*-martingale f with $f \geq 1/2$ and $E^*[f_T] = 1$ by

$$f := 1 + N/2a$$

where a>0 is given by $a := \| \sup_{s \leq T} |N_s| \|_{\infty}$. f defines an equivalent martingale measure $\tilde{P}^*$ via

$$\tilde{P}^*(F) := \int_F f_T \, dP^* \qquad \forall F \in \mathcal{F}\ .$$

The martingale property results from

$$E^*[f_t\, S_t^k | F_s] = E^*[S_t^k | F_s] + \frac{1}{2a}\, E^*[N_t\, S_t^k | F_s] \tag{4.2.6}$$

$$= S_s^k + \frac{1}{2a}\, N_s\, S_s^k$$

$$= f_s\, S_s^k \qquad P^* \text{ a.s.} \quad \forall\, k \in \{1,\dots,K\}$$

Thus

$$E^*[N_T\, X] = 2a\; E^*[f_T\, X] - 2a\; E^*[X] = 0 \;,$$

which yields the assertion, since

$$E^{Q}[X] = E^*[M_T X] = E^*[X] + E^*[N_T X] \quad .$$

(ii) Now suppose (4.2.5) holds true. Consider $N \in L(N^n)$. N is of the form $N = \int \phi \, dN^n$, where ϕ fulfills the usual integrability condition. There exists a sequence $(\phi_m)_{m \in \mathbb{N}}$ of simple integrands with $N^m := \int \phi_m \, dN^n \to N$ in $H^2(P^*)$. All N^m are bounded.
In analogy to (i) we get

$$E^*[N_T\, X] = \lim E^*[N_T^m\, X] = 0 .$$

Now consider $N \in L(N^1,\dots,N^n)$. This yields

$$N = \sum_{i=1}^{n} \int \phi^i \, dN^i$$

and

$$E^*[N_T\, X] = \sum_{i=1}^{n} E^*[(\int_0^T \phi^i \, dN^i) X] = 0 .$$

Since N is the closure in $H^2(P^*)$ of $\bigcup_{n \in \mathbb{N}} L(N^1,\dots,N^n)$

$$E^*[N_T X] = 0$$

holds true for every $N \in \mathcal{N}$. Thus we get

$$\begin{aligned} E^Q[X] &= E^*[M_T X] \\ &= E^*[X] + E^*[N_T X] \\ &= E^*[X] \quad \square \end{aligned}$$

4.3 Classes of P^*-attainable contingent claims for specific security price processes

For the securities market models considered in Section 3.3 the classes of P^*-attainable contingent claims are determined in this section. Simultaneously, preference-free valuation formulas are obtained for those contingent claims.

4.3.1 Geometric Brownian motion

We consider the securities market model introduced in Section 3.3.1. Example 4.1.8 shows that the contingent claim $(S_T^1 - K)^+$ is P-attainable in this model. This is achieved by determining a selffinancing generating trading strategy. Since $(S_T^1 - K)^+$ represents the time T value of a European call option written on a stock with price process (3.3.1), with expiration date T and exercise price K, a European call option can be generated by a selffinancing portfolio in the bond and the given stock. Thus its preference-free valuation is given by E[X]. Now it will be shown that every contingent claim is P-attainable in this model for all $P \in \mathbb{P}(S)$. This implies that for valuation purposes a derivation like the one of Example 4.1.8 is not necessary.

Because of Theorem 4.2.4 it suffices to show that $\mathbb{Q}(S) = \{P\}$. In doing this, we will use the fact that

$$L_P(S^o, W) = H^2(P) \quad ^{1)} \tag{4.3.1}$$

holds (cf. ELLIOTT (1982), Theorem 12.33, p. 146).

Note that S^1 is the solution of

$$S_t^1 = S_o^1 + \int_o^t \sigma S_s^1 \, dW_s \qquad \forall\, t \in [0,T] \,. \tag{4.3.2}$$

This can easily be shown using the exponential formula (cf. the Appendix), i.e. we have

$$S^1 = S_o^1 \, E(\int \sigma \, dW) \,. \tag{4.3.3}$$

$E(\int \sigma \, dW)$ is the solution of (4.3.2), since it is continuous and $(\int \sigma \, dW)_o = 0$ holds true.

Since S^1 is strictly positive, $\frac{1}{S^1}$ is defined. S^1 and $\frac{1}{S^1}$ are locally bounded as cadlag and predictable processes. Then the standard properties of the stochastic integral for locally bounded integrands (cf. DELLACHERIE/MEYER (1982), Theorem 3, p. 313 and p. 320, 9) imply

$$\int_0^T \frac{1}{(S_u^1)^2} \, d[S^1, S^1]_u = \int_0^T \frac{1}{(S_u^1)^2} \, d([S_o^1 + \int \sigma S^1 dW \,,\, S_o^1 + \int \sigma S^1 dW])$$

$$= 1 + \int_0^T \frac{1}{(S_u^1)^2} \, d[\int \sigma S^1 dW \,,\, \int \sigma S^1 dW]_u$$

$$= 1 + \int_0^T \frac{1}{(S_u^1)^2} \, \sigma^2 \, (S_u^1)^2 \, d[W,W]_u$$

$$= 1 + \int_0^T \sigma^2 \, du$$

$$= 1 + \sigma^2 T < \infty \,.$$

---

1) Remember that $S^o \equiv 1$, i.e. S^o in (4.3.1) represents the constant martingale of value 1. In the literature, this martingale is also denoted by 1 (cf. JACOD (1979), pp. 116).

Thus the stochastic integral $\int \frac{1}{S^1} dS^1$ is defined, and, since all integrands considered are locally bounded, we get

$$W_t = \int_0^t dW_u$$

$$= \frac{1}{\sigma} \int_0^t \frac{1}{S^1} \sigma S^1 \, dW$$

$$= \frac{1}{\sigma} \int_0^t \frac{1}{S^1} \, d(\int \sigma S^1 dW)$$

$$= \frac{1}{\sigma} \int_0^t \frac{1}{S^1} \, d(S^1 - S^1_0)$$

$$= \frac{1}{\sigma} (\int_0^t \frac{1}{S^1} \, dS^1 - 1)$$

for all $t \in [0,T]$, yielding $W \in L(S^1)$, since $S^1_0 > 0$ implies $S^0 \in L(S^1)$. This results in

$$L(S^0,W) \subset L(S^1) ,$$

and $L(S^1) = H^2(P)$ follows from (4.3.1).

Now consider $Q \in \mathbb{Q}(S)$. Let $M_T := \frac{dQ}{dP}$ denote the Radon-Nikodym derivative of Q with respect to P and $M := (M_t)_{t \in [0,T]}$ the P-martingale defined by $M_t := E[M_T | F_t]$. $N := M-1$ is a P-martingale with $N_0 = M_0 - 1 = 0$ (since $Q(\Omega) = 1$), and $NS^1 = MS^1 - S^1$ is a martingale with respect to P. Thus we get

$$N \in (L(S^1))^{\perp} = (H^2(P))^{\perp} = \{0\}.$$

It follows that $Q = P$. Since $\mathbb{Q}(S) = \mathbb{P}(S) = \{P\}$, every contingent claim X is P-attainable. Its price is given by $E[X]$.

4.3.2 A process with a random variance

The securities market model introduced in Section 3.3.2 is considered. We will determine the class of P^*-attainable contingent claims in this model. Note that the filtration defined in 3.3.2 fulfills the usual conditions. The characterization of attainability of Theorem 4.2.4 is used and the following set is considered.

$$\mathbb{P}_o(S^1) := \{P_\theta \mid P_\theta(F) := \int_F f_\theta \, dP^* \quad \forall F \in \mathcal{F},$$

$$f_\theta(\omega) := \frac{\theta}{\theta^*} 1_A(\omega) + \frac{1-\theta}{1-\theta^*} 1_{A^c}(\omega), \; \theta \in (0,1)\} \tag{4.3.4}$$

It is easily seen that P_θ, $\theta \in (0,1)$, defined in (4.3.4) are probability measures with the properties $P_\theta(G \times \Omega_2) = P(G)$, $\forall G \in \mathcal{G}$ and $P_\theta(A) = \theta$. All P_θ are equivalent with bounded Radon-Nikodym derivatives with respect to each other. The martingale property of S^1 with respect to $((\Omega, \mathcal{F}, P_\theta), \mathbb{F})$ follows easily using the stochastic independence of W and 1_A under P_θ. Thus

$$\mathbb{P}_o(S^1) \subset \mathbb{P}(S^1) \tag{4.3.5}$$

holds true.

In Lemma 4.3.2 it will be shown that the elements of $\mathbb{P}_o(S^1)$ are in a certain sense the simplest equivalent martingale measures of S^1.

First of all, however, we will check whether the contingent claim $X = (S_T^1 - K)^+$ is P^*-attainable in this model, i.e. whether a European call option can be generated selffinancingly by a portfolio in a riskless bond and the stock. The following lemma shows that this is not the case.

4.3.1 Lemma

Consider the securities market model of Section 3.3.2 with the price process S^1 of the form (3.3.3). The contingent claim $X := (S_T^1 - K)^+$ is not P^*-attainable.

Proof:

The criterion of Theorem 4.2.4 will be used. For that purpose we will determine the expected value of $(S_T^1 - K)^+$ with respect to all probability measures $P_\theta \in \mathbb{P}_o(S^1)$, which is denoted by $E_\theta[(S_T^1 - K)^+]$. We use the notation introduced in Example 4.1.8 as well as

$$Y_T^1 := S_o^1 \exp\left(\sigma_o W_{t_o} - \frac{\sigma_o^2}{2} t_o + \sigma_1 (W_T - W_{t_o}) - \frac{\sigma_1^2}{2}(T - t_o)\right)$$

$$Y_T^2 := S_o^1 \exp\left(\sigma_o W_{t_o} - \frac{\sigma_o^2}{2} t_o + \sigma_2 (W_T - W_{t_o}) - \frac{\sigma_2^2}{2}(T - t_o)\right)$$

$$\sigma_3 := \sqrt{(\sigma_o^2 - \sigma_1^2)t_o + \sigma_1^2 T}$$

$$\sigma_4 := \sqrt{(\sigma_o^2 - \sigma_2^2)t_o + \sigma_2^2 T} \quad .$$

The random variables $\ln Y_T^1$ and $\ln Y_T^2$ are normally distributed with mean $\ln S_o^1 - \frac{\sigma_3^2}{2}$ and $\ln S_o^1 - \frac{\sigma_4^2}{2}$, respectively, and variance σ_3^2 and σ_4^2, respectively. Using the stochastic independence of the increments of Brownian motion and the stochastic independence of the random variables 1_A and W_t as well as (4.1.12) and (4.1.13) we get

$$E_\theta[(S_T^1 - K)^+] = \int_{\{S_T^1 > K\}} S_T^1 dP_\theta - KP_\theta(\{S_T^1 > K\})$$

$$= \int_{\{S_T^1>K\}} 1_A Y_T^1 \, dP_\theta + \int_{\{S_T^1>K\}} 1_{A^c} Y_T^2 dP_\theta - KP_\theta(\{S_T^1>K\} \cap A)$$

$$- KP_\theta(\{S_T^1 > K\} \cap A^c)$$

$$= \int_{\{Y_T^1>K\}} 1_A Y_T^1 \, dP_\theta - KP_\theta(\{Y_T^1 > K\} \cap A)$$

$$+ \int_{\{Y_T^2>K\}} 1_{A^c} Y_T^2 \, dP_\theta - KP_\theta(\{Y_T^2>K\} \cap A^c)$$

$$= \theta(E_\theta[Y_T^1 1_{\{Y_T^1 > K\}}] - KP_\theta(\{Y_T^1 > K\}))$$

$$+ (1-\theta)(E_\theta[Y_T^2 1_{\{Y_T^2 > K\}}] - KP_\theta(\{Y_T^2 > K\}))$$

$$= \theta(S_o^1 \Phi(\frac{\ln \frac{S_o^1}{K} + \frac{\sigma_3^2}{2}}{\sigma_3}) - K\Phi(\frac{\ln \frac{S_o^1}{K} - \frac{\sigma_3^2}{2}}{\sigma_3}))$$

$$+ (1-\theta)(S_o^1 \Phi(\frac{\ln \frac{S_o^1}{K} + \frac{\sigma_4^2}{2}}{\sigma_4}) - K\Phi(\frac{\ln \frac{S_o^1}{K} - \frac{\sigma_4^2}{2}}{\sigma_4}))$$

$E_\theta[(S_T^1 - K)^+]$ is constant on $\mathbb{P}_o(S^1)$ if and only if

$$S_o^1 \Phi(\frac{\ln \frac{S_o^1}{K} + \frac{\sigma_3^2}{2}}{\sigma_3}) - K\Phi(\frac{\ln \frac{S_o^1}{K} - \frac{\sigma_3^2}{2}}{\sigma_3}) - S_o^1 \Phi(\frac{\ln \frac{S_o^1}{K} + \frac{\sigma_4^2}{2}}{\sigma_4})$$

$$+ K\Phi(\frac{\ln \frac{S_o^1}{K} - \frac{\sigma_4^2}{2}}{\sigma_4}) = 0$$

holds true. We consider the function $f : \mathbb{R}_{++} \to \mathbb{R}$ defined by

$$f(K) := S_o^1 \Phi(\frac{\ln \frac{S_o^1}{K} + \frac{\sigma_3^2}{2}}{\sigma_3}) - K\Phi(\frac{\ln \frac{S_o^1}{K} - \frac{\sigma_3^2}{2}}{\sigma_3}) - S_o^1 \Phi(\frac{\ln \frac{S_o^1}{K} + \frac{\sigma_4^2}{2}}{\sigma_4})$$

$$+ K\Phi(\frac{\ln \frac{S_o^1}{K} - \frac{\sigma_4^2}{2}}{\sigma_4}) .$$

f is continuously differentiable. Making use of the relationship

$$K\,n\left(\frac{\ln\frac{S_o^1}{K}-\frac{\sigma_i^2}{2}}{\sigma_i}\right) = S_o^1\,n\left(\frac{\ln\frac{S_o^1}{K}+\frac{\sigma_i^2}{2}}{\sigma_i}\right) \qquad i=3,4$$

we get

$$f'(K) = S_o^1\,n\left(\frac{\ln\frac{S_o^1}{K}+\frac{\sigma_3^2}{2}}{\sigma_3}\right)\left(-\frac{1}{K\sigma_3}\right) - \Phi\left(\frac{\ln\frac{S_o^1}{K}-\frac{\sigma_3^2}{2}}{\sigma_3}\right)$$

$$- K\,n\left(\frac{\ln\frac{S_o^1}{K}-\frac{\sigma_3^2}{2}}{\sigma_3}\right)\left(-\frac{1}{K\sigma_3}\right) - S_o^1\,n\left(\frac{\ln\frac{S_o^1}{K}+\frac{\sigma_4^2}{2}}{\sigma_4}\right)\left(-\frac{1}{K\sigma_4}\right)$$

$$+ \Phi\left(\frac{\ln\frac{S_o^1}{K}-\frac{\sigma_4^2}{2}}{\sigma_4}\right) + K\,n\left(\frac{\ln\frac{S_o^1}{K}-\frac{\sigma_4^2}{2}}{\sigma_4}\right)\left(-\frac{1}{K\sigma_4}\right)$$

$$= -\Phi\left(\frac{\ln\frac{S_o^1}{K}-\frac{\sigma_3^2}{2}}{\sigma_3}\right) + \Phi\left(\frac{\ln\frac{S_o^1}{K}-\frac{\sigma_4^2}{2}}{\sigma_4}\right)$$

and

$$f''(K) = -n\left(\frac{\ln\frac{S_o^1}{K}-\frac{\sigma_3^2}{2}}{\sigma_3}\right)\left(-\frac{1}{K\sigma_3}\right) + n\left(\frac{\ln\frac{S_o^1}{K}-\frac{\sigma_4^2}{2}}{\sigma_4}\right)\left(-\frac{1}{K\sigma_4}\right)$$

$$= \frac{1}{K\sigma_3}\,n\left(\frac{\ln\frac{S_o^1}{K}-\frac{\sigma_3^2}{2}}{\sigma_3}\right) - \frac{1}{K\sigma_4}\,n\left(\frac{\ln\frac{S_o^1}{K}-\frac{\sigma_4^2}{2}}{\sigma_4}\right)$$

$f'(K) = 0$ yields $K_o := S_o^1 \exp\left(\frac{1}{2}\sigma_3\sigma_4\right)$, and we have $f''(K_o) > 0$ if $\sigma_3 < \sigma_4$ and $f''(K_o) < 0$ if $\sigma_3 > \sigma_4$. We consider the case $\sigma_3 < \sigma_4$. Then f has a minimum at K_o with

$$f(K_o) = S_o^1 \left(\Phi\left(\frac{\ln \frac{S_o^1}{K_o} + \frac{\sigma_3^2}{2}}{\sigma_3}\right) - \Phi\left(\frac{\ln \frac{S_o^1}{K_o} + \frac{\sigma_4^2}{2}}{\sigma_4}\right)\right)$$

$$= S_o^1 \left(\Phi\left(\frac{\ln \frac{S_o^1}{K_o} - \frac{\sigma_3^2}{2}}{\sigma_3} + \sigma_3\right) - \Phi\left(\frac{\ln \frac{S_o^1}{K_o} - \frac{\sigma_3^2}{2}}{\sigma_3} + \sigma_4\right)\right) < 0$$

and $f'(K) < 0$ if $K \in (0,K_o)$ and $f'(K) > 0$ if $K \in (K_o,\infty)$, i.e. f is strictly decreasing on $(0,K_o)$ and strictly increasing on (K_o,∞). Furthermore,

$$\lim_{K\to 0} f(K) = \lim_{K\to\infty} f(K) = 0 .$$

This implies $f(K) < 0$ for all K. To see this, assume the existence of a $K_1 \in (0,\infty)$ with $\gamma := f(K_1) \geq 0$. We have $K_1 \in (0,K_o)$ or $K_1 \in (K_o,\infty)$. In the first case choose $n_o \in \mathbb{N}$ such that $1/n_o < K_1$. This yields the following contradiction

$$0 = \lim_{K\to 0} f(K) = \lim_{n\geq n_o} f(\tfrac{1}{n}) \geq f(\tfrac{1}{n_o}) > f(K_1) \geq 0 .$$

In the second case choose a $n_o \in \mathbb{N}$ such that $n_o > K_1$. This yields the following contradiction

$$0 = \lim_{K\to\infty} f(K) = \lim_{n\geq n_o} f(n) \geq f(n_o) > f(K_1) \geq 0 .$$

In the case $\sigma_3 > \sigma_4$ one concludes similarly and one can show that $f(K) > 0$ for all $K \in \mathbb{R}_{++}$ holds true. Summing up, $E_\theta[(S_T^1 - K)^+]$ is constant for $P_\theta \in \mathbb{P}_o(S^1)$ if and only if $\sigma_3 = \sigma_4$. This is equivalent to $\sigma_1 = \sigma_2$, which has been excluded. □

<u>Remark</u>

In Chapter 5 it will be shown that in the case $\sigma_1 = \sigma_2$ $\Phi(S^1) = \mathbb{P}(S^1) = \{P_{\theta^*}\}$ holds true.

Now the set $\mathbb{Q}(S)$ of P^*-continuous signed martingale measures will be determined. Before getting into this, the subspace of purely discontinuous martingales has to be introduced. $H_0^{2,c}(P^*)$ denotes the set of all continuous martingales M with $M_0 = 0$ P^* a.s. It can be shown that $H_0^{2,c}(P^*)$ is a stable subspace of $H^2(P^*)$, i.e. $H_0^{2,c}(P^*)$ has the properties given in Lemma 4.2.1. Its strongly orthogonal complement $H^{2,d}(P^*) := (H_0^{2,c}(P^*))^{\perp}$, which is defined in analogy to (4.2.3), also is a stable subspace of $H^2(P^*)$. Elements of $H^{2,d}(P^*)$ are called *purely discontinuous martingales*. We have $H^2(P^*) = H_0^{2,c}(P^*) \oplus H^{2,d}(P^*)$, i.e. every element $M \in H^2(P^*)$ has a unique decomposition $M = M^1 + M^2$ with $M^1 \in H_0^{2,c}(P^*)$ and $M^2 \in H^{2,d}(P^*)$. (See for example ELLIOTT (1982), pp. 88 and the Appendix.) $H_0^{2,d}(P^*)$ denotes the set of martingales $N \in H^{2,d}(P^*)$ with $N_0 = 0$.

With those definitions we arrive at

4.3.2 Lemma

The set $\mathbb{Q}(S)$ of P^*-continuous signed martingale measures for the securities market model of Section 3.3.2 is given by

$$\mathbb{Q}(S) := \{Q \mid Q(F) := \int_F M_T \, dP^*, \; M_T \in L^2(P^*) \, , \tag{4.3.6}$$

$$E^*[M_T] = 1 \; , \; N := M - 1 \in H_0^{2,d}(P^*)\} \; .$$

Proof:

It is easily seen that S^1 is a continuous martingale. By JACOD (1979), p. 45, (2.46), we get for every $M \in L(S^1)$

$$\Delta M_t = \Delta(\int \phi \, dS)_t = \phi_t \, \Delta S_t \; ,$$

i.e. all $M \in L(S^1)$ are continuous martingales. Consider Q with

$$Q(F) := \int_F M_T \, dP^* \, , \; M_T \in L^2(P^*) \; , \; E^*[M_T] = 1 \; \text{ and } N := M - 1 \in H_0^{2,d}(P^*) .$$

Q is a P^*-continuous martingale measure. The martingale property results as follows. $S^1 - S^1_o$ is an element of $H^{2,c}_o(P^*)$. By definition of $H^{2,d}_o(P^*)$, $(S^1 - S^1_o)N$ is a P^* martingale. This is also true for $S^1_o N$, since $N_o = 0$ P^* a.s. by assumption. Thus

$$S^1 M = S^1 N + S^1 = (S^1 - S^1_o)N + S^1_o N + S^1$$

is a P^* martingale since it is the sum of three P^* martingales.

Let Q be a P^*-continuous martingale measure. M_T denotes the Radon-Nikodym derivative of Q with respect to P^*. We have $E^*[M_T^2] < \infty$ and $E^*[M_T] = 1$. M denotes the P^*-martingale consisting of $M_t := E^*[M_T | F_t]$ and N the P^*-martingale $N := M-1$. It has to be shown that $N \in H^{2,d}_o(P^*)$. N has a unique decomposition

$$N = N^c + N^d \quad \text{with } N^c \in H^{2,c}_o(P^*) \text{ and } N^d \in H^{2,d}_o(P^*) .$$

The continuity of S^1 implies that $(S^1 - S^1_o)N^d$ is a martingale with respect to P^* and this is also true for

$$N^c S^1 = NS^1 - N^d S^1 = MS^1 - S^1 - N^d(S^1 - S^1_o) - N^d S^1_o .$$

It will be shown that $N^c = 0$. Using Fubini's theorem and the continuity of S^1, it follows almost immediately that the strong orthogonality of N^c and S^1 implies the strong orthogonality of the ω_{2i}-sections $N^c_{\omega_{2i}}$ and $S^1_{\omega_{2i}}$, i=1,2. $S^1_{\omega_{2i}}$ is of the form

$$(S_{\omega_{2i}})_t = 1_{[0,t_o]} S^1_o \exp\left(\sigma_o \tilde{W}_t - \frac{\sigma_o^2}{2} t\right) \tag{4.3.7}$$

$$+ 1_{(t_o,T]} S^1_o \exp\left(\sigma_o \tilde{W}_{t_o} - \frac{\sigma_o^2}{2} t_o + \sigma_i (\tilde{W}_t - \tilde{W}_{t_o}) - \frac{\sigma_i^2}{2}(t - t_o)\right),$$

i=1,2, where $\tilde{W}_t$ denotes the ω_{2i}-section of W_t. By the exponential formula it follows that $S_{\omega_{21}}$ is the solution of

$$Z_t = Z_o + \int_o^t Z_{s-} dR \tag{4.3.8}$$

for $R := \int \tau_1 \, d\widetilde{W}$ with

$$\tau_1 := \sigma_o 1_{[0,t_o]} + \sigma_1 1_{(t_o,T]} .$$

As in 4.3.1 one concludes that

$$L_P(S^1_{\omega_{21}}) = H^2(P)$$

holds. This implies $N^c_{\omega_{21}} = 0$. Similarly, one obtains $N^c_{\omega_{22}} = 0$, which yields the assertion. □

Having obtained the set $\Phi(S)$, the class of P^*-attainable contingent claims is determined. We get

4.3.3 Lemma

A contingent claim X is P^*-attainable if and only if the martingale $(X_t) := (E^*[X|F_t])$ has a continuous modification.

Remark

The continuity of the martingale (X_t) is equivalent to

$$E[X_{\omega_{21}} | G_{t_o}] = E[X_{\omega_{22}} | G_{t_o}] . \tag{4.3.9}$$

Proof

It remains to show that every continuous martingale (X_t) is an element of $L_{P^*}(S^1)$. Consider $X - X_o$. Then $(X_t - X_o)_{t\in[0,T]}$ is an element of $H^{2,c}_o(P^*)$ and for all $N \in H^{2,d}(P^*)$ we have

$$E^*[(X - X_o)N_T] = 0 .$$

Thus we obtain for all $N \in H^{2,d}(P^*)$

$$E^*[X(N_T - N_o)] = 0$$

which results for all $N \in H^{2,d}_o(P^*)$ in

$E^*[XN_T] = 0$.

With $(L_{P^*}(S^1))^{\perp} = H_0^{2,d}(P^*)$, Lemma 4.2.2(f) and Lemma 4.2.3 we get the P^*-attainability of X. □

Now some examples of P^*-attainable contingent claims will be given.

4.3.4 Example

Using the criterion of Lemma 4.3.3 we get the P^*-attainability of every $G_T \otimes \{\emptyset, \Omega_2\}$ measurable contingent claim. That means that every contingent claim that is attainable, if the security price process follows a geometric Brownian motion, is P^*-attainable.

4.3.5 Example

A further example of a P^*-attainable contingent claim is given by

$$X = 1_A \exp((W_T - W_{t_0}) - \tfrac{1}{2}(T - t_0)) + 1_{A^C} \exp(2(W_T - W_{t_0}) - 2(T - t_0)).$$

In fact, every security with a price process of the form (3.3.3) for arbitrary σ_i, i=0,1,2 is P^*-attainable in this model.

The following example shows that in order to check whether or not a contingent claim is P^*-attainable, the set $\mathbb{P}_0(S^1)$ does not suffice.

4.3.6 Example

Consider the contingent claim

$$X := 1_A \exp(W_T - \tfrac{T}{2}) + 1_{A^C} \exp(2W_T - 2T).$$

We get

$$\begin{aligned} E_\theta[X] &= \theta E_\theta[\exp(W_T - \tfrac{T}{2})] + (1 - \theta)E_\theta[\exp(2W_T - 2T)] \\ &= 1 \end{aligned}$$

for all $P_\theta \in \mathbb{P}_o(S^1)$ and

$$E_\theta[\exp(W_T - \frac{T}{2}) | F_{t_o}] - E_\theta[\exp(2W_T - 2T) | F_{t_o}]$$

$$= \exp(W_{t_o} - \frac{t_o}{2}) - \exp(2W_{t_o} - 2t_o) \quad .$$

X is not P^*-attainable, since (X_t) does not have a continuous modification.

4.3.3 Geometric Poisson process

Consider the security price process given in 3.3.3. In analogy to Example 4.1.8 it can be shown that the contingent claim $X = (S^1_T - K)^+$ is P-attainable by determining a selffinancing trading strategy. Now we will show that every contingent claim is P-attainable in this model. For that purpose it will first be shown that the security price process given in (3.3.4) is the exponential of the process $R_t := (\exp(1) - 1)(N_t - \lambda t)$. Using the fact that N only has jumps of a magnitude of 1 (cf. ELLIOTT (1982), p. 143, Theorem 12.31) the exponential formula results in

$$\mathcal{E}(R)_t = S^1_o (\exp R_t) \prod_{0<s\leq t} ((1 + \Delta R_s) \exp(-\Delta R_s))$$

$$= S^1_o (\exp R_t) \prod_{0<s\leq t} ((1 + (\exp(1) - 1)\Delta N_s) \exp(-(\exp(1) - 1)\Delta N_s))$$

$$= S^1_o (\exp R_t) \exp((-\exp(1) + 2) N_t)$$

$$= S^1_o \exp(N_t - \lambda(\exp(1) - 1)t) \quad .$$

Now we consider processes $(X_t)_{t \in \mathcal{T}(\lambda)}$ with index set $\mathcal{T}(\lambda) = [0, \frac{T}{\lambda}]$. This will be expressed by the index $[0, \frac{T}{\lambda}]$ in the following derivation. By ELLIOTT (1982), p. 146, Theorem 12.35, we have

$$\mathcal{L}(S^o, N^1) = \mathcal{H}^2(P)_{[o, \frac{T}{\lambda}]} \qquad (4.3.10)$$

The martingale N^1 is defined by $N^1_t := M_t - t$, where M denotes a Poisson process with parameter 1. Define $\tau = (\tau_t)_{t \in [o,T]}$ by $\tau_t := \lambda t$. τ is a change of time and we have (cf. JACOD (1979), p. 318, (10.19))

$$\mathcal{L}(S^o, N^\lambda) = \mathcal{H}^2(P)_{[o,T]} \qquad (4.3.11)$$

for N^λ with $N^\lambda_t := N - \lambda t$.

Now one concludes similar to 4.3.3. S^1 is the solution of the equation

$$S^1_t = S^1_o + \int_o^t S^1_{s-} \, dR_s \; .$$

Since $S^1 > 0$,

$$\phi_t := \begin{cases} \dfrac{1}{S^1_{t-}} & t > 0 \\ 0 & t = 0 \end{cases}$$

is well-defined and predictable. Since all integrands are locally bounded, we obtain

$$\int_o^T \phi_t^2 \, d[S^1, S^1]_t = \int_o^T \phi_t^2 (S^1_{t-})^2 \, d[R,R]_t$$

$$= [R,R]_T \qquad .$$

This implies that $\int \phi \, dS^1$ is defined and one concludes as in 4.3.1 that

$$\mathcal{L}(S^1) = \mathcal{H}^2(P)$$

holds. Again as in 4.3.1 $\mathbb{Q}(S) = \{P\}$ follows. Every contingent claim X is P-attainable and its price is given by E[X].

4.4 The relationship between P*-attainable contingent claims and solutions of associated difference-differential equations

This section examines the relationship between P*-attainable contingent claims and the solutions of special associated difference-differential equations. It serves to bridge the gap between the method of valuation proposed in this monograph and the method of valuation by means of difference-differential equations which can be found in the literature (cf. BLACK/SCHOLES (1973), MERTON (1973), COX/ROSS (1976a),(1976b) MERTON (1976b), SMITH (1976), BRENNAN/SCHWARTZ (1977),MERTON (1977), BRENNAN/SCHWARTZ (1978),(1979),FEIGER/JACQUILLAT (1979),GESKE (1979a),(1979b), GOLDMAN/SOSIN/GATTO (1979), SMITH (1979), STULZ (1982)). It has to be emphasized, however, that the valuation method proposed in this monograph is the more general one. The valuation method by means of difference-differential equations assumes a functional relationship of the contingent claim X of the form

$$X_t = E^*[X|\mathcal{F}_t] = f(t,S_t^1,\dots,S_t^K) \qquad \forall\, t \in [0,T] \,, \tag{4.4.1}$$

where f is twice continuously differentiable. In contrast to this no differentiability assumptions are needed for the valuation method proposed in this monograph. More than that, no restrictions such as (4.4.1) are required. More complicated relationships are allowed for. If the assumptions of the differential-difference valuation method are fulfilled, however, both methods yield the same result. First of all, Theorem 4.4.1 will give a sufficient condition of P*-attainability. For continuous security price processes this condition is also necessary as will be shown in Theorem 4.4.2 below.

4.4.1 Theorem

Let X be a contingent claim that fulfills (4.4.1), where $f : [0,T]\times \mathbb{R}^K \to \mathbb{R}$ is of class C^2. Assume that the following conditions hold true

$$E^*[\int_0^T (\frac{\partial f}{\partial S^k}(s,S_{s-}^1,\dots,S_{s-}^K))^2\, d\,[S^k,S^k]_s] < \infty \tag{4.4.2}$$

$$\forall\, k \in \{1,\dots,K\}$$

$$\int_0^t \frac{\partial f}{\partial s}(s,S_{s-}^1,\dots,S_{s-}^K)ds +$$

$$+ \frac{1}{2}\sum_{k,l=1}^{K}\int_0^t \frac{\partial^2 f}{\partial S^k \partial S^l}(s,S_{s-}^1,\dots,S_{s-}^K)\, d[S^k - S_0^k, S^l - S_0^l]^c$$

$$+ \sum_{0<s\le t}(X_s - f(s,S_{s-}^1,\dots,S_{s-}^K) \qquad (4.4.3)$$

$$- \sum_{k=1}^{K}(\frac{\partial f}{\partial S^k}(s,S_{s-}^1,\dots,S_{s-}^K))\,\Delta S_s^k) = 0$$

$$\forall\, t \in [0,T],$$

Then X is P^*- attainable.

Proof

First of all, Ito's lemma yields

$$X_t = X_0 + \int_0^t \frac{\partial f}{\partial s}(s,S_{s-}^1,\dots,S_{s-}^K)ds$$

$$+ \sum_{k=1}^{K}\int_0^t \frac{\partial f}{\partial S^k}(s,S_{s-}^1,\dots,S_{s-}^K)\, d(S^k - S_0^k) \qquad (4.4.4)$$

$$+ \frac{1}{2}\sum_{k,l=1}^{K}\int_0^t \frac{\partial^2 f}{\partial S^k \partial S^l}(s,S_{s-}^1,\dots,S_{s-}^K)\, d[S^k - S_0^k, S^l - S_0^l]^c$$

$$+ \sum_{0<s\le t}(X_s - f(s,S_{s-}^1,\dots,S_{s-}^K)$$

$$- \sum_{k=1}^{K}(\frac{\partial f}{\partial S^k}(s,S_{s-}^1,\dots,S_{s-}^K)\,\Delta S_s^k)).$$

$\frac{\partial f}{\partial S^k}(\cdot,S_-^1,\dots,S_-^K)$ is predictable and fulfills the integrability condition for the existence of the stochastic integral. By Lemma 4.2.3

the P^*-attainability of X follows, because of (4.4.3).

4.4.2 Theorem

Let X be a contingent claim that fulfills (4.4.1), where $f : [0,T] \times \mathbb{R}^K \to \mathbb{R}$ is of class C^2. Furthermore, all S^k, $k \in \{1,\dots,K\}$, are assumed to be continuous, and (4.4.2) is assumed to hold. X is P^*-attainable if and only if

$$\int_0^t \frac{\partial f}{\partial s} ds + \frac{1}{2} \sum_{k=1}^{K} \int_0^t \frac{\partial^2 f}{(\partial S^k)^2} d[S^k - S_0^k, S^k - S_0^k] = 0 \qquad (4.4.5)$$

$$\forall\, t \in [0,T]$$

holds true.

Proof:

Note that (4.4.3) reduces to (4.4.5) for continuous processes S^k. Furthermore, because of (4.1.3) for all $k \neq l$, $k,l \in \{1,\dots,K\}$ we have

$$[S^k - S_0^k, S^l - S_0^l] = 0 \; .$$

Let X be P^*-attainable. There exist ϕ^k, $k \in \{1,\dots,K\}$ with

$E^*[\int_0^T (\phi^k)^2 \, d[S^k,S^k]] < \infty$, such that

$$X_t = X_0 + \sum_{k=1}^{K} \int_0^t \phi^k \, d(S^k - S_0^k) \qquad \forall\, t \in [0,T]$$

holds true. Ito's lemma yields

$$X_t = X_0 + \sum_{k=1}^{K} \int_0^t \frac{\partial f}{\partial S^k} d(S^k - S_0^k)$$

$$+ \int_0^t \frac{\partial f}{\partial s} ds + \frac{1}{2} \sum_{k=1}^{K} \int_0^t \frac{\partial^2 f}{(\partial S^k)^2} d[S^k - S_0^k, S^k - S_0^k]$$

The two representations of X_t imply

$$\sum_{k=1}^{K} \int_0^t (\phi^k - \frac{\partial f}{\partial S^k})\, d(S^k - S_o^k) \tag{4.4.6}$$

$$= \int_0^t \frac{\partial f}{\partial s}\, ds + \frac{1}{2} \sum_{k=1}^{K} \int_0^t \frac{\partial^2 f}{(\partial S^k)^2}\, d[S^k - S_o^k, S^k - S_o^k] \ .$$

The expression on the left-hand side of (4.4.6) is a continuous square integrable martingale, the expression on the right-hand side is a continuous process of bounded variation (cf. DELLACHERIE/MEYER (1982), p. 333, 25). Thus the martingale on the left-hand side of (4.4.6) is predictable and of bounded variation. By ELLIOTT (1982), p. 121, Lemma 11.39(ii) it is equal to a constant. Because of

$$\left(\sum_{k=1}^{K} \int_0^t (\phi^k - \frac{\partial f}{\partial S^k})\, d(S^k - S_o^k) \right)_o = 0$$

this constant has to be zero, yielding (4.4.5). □

The relationship between the partial derivatives of the function f and trading strategies that generate a P*-attainable contingent claim is described in the following corollary.

4.4.3 Corollary

We take up the assumptions of Theorem 4.4.1. The P*-attainable contingent claim X is generated by the self-financing trading strategy ϕ defined by

$$\phi_t^o := E[X] - \sum_{k=1}^{K} \phi_o^k S_o^k + \sum_{k=1}^{K} (\int \phi^k dS^k)_{t-} - \sum_{k=1}^{K} \phi_t^k S_{t-}^k \qquad \forall t \in [0,T]$$

$$\phi_t^k := \frac{\partial f}{\partial S^k}(t, S_{t-}^1, \ldots, S_{t-}^K) \qquad k \in \{1,\ldots,K\},\ \forall\, t \in [0,T]$$

Remarks

1. Assumption (4.4.2) is essential. Without this assumption only the local boundedness of $\frac{\partial f}{\partial S^k}(\cdot,S^1_-,\ldots,S^K_-)$ can be ensured. In this case, the process

$$\int \frac{\partial f}{\partial S^k}(s,S^1_{s-},\ldots,S^K_{s-})\,d(S^k-S^k_o)_s$$

is a local martingale.

2. In general, it cannot be expected that (4.4.3) is a necessary condition for P^*-attainability of a contingent claim of the form (4.4.1). This is due to the fact that although every P^*-attainable contingent claim is a special semimartingale and thus has a unique decomposition into a constant, a local martingale and a predictable process of bounded variation (cf. DELLACHERIE/MEYER (1982), p. 213, Remark 24(c)), in general (4.4.4) is not of this form.

A further corollary to Theorem 4.4.2 follows.

4.4.4 Corollary

Let the assumptions to Theorem 4.4.2 be fulfilled. Furthermore there are K positive Borel functions g^k on $[0,T]\times\mathbb{R}^K$ such that

$$[S^k-S^k_o,S^k-S^k_o]_t = \int_0^t g^k(s,S^1_s,\ldots,S^K_s)\,ds \qquad \forall k\in\{1,\ldots,K\}. \tag{4.4.7}$$

If f fulfills the partial differential equation

$$\frac{\partial f}{\partial t}+\frac{1}{2}\sum_{k=1}^{K}\frac{\partial^2 f}{(\partial S^k)^2}(t,S^1_t,\ldots,S^K_t)\,g^k(t,S^1_t,\ldots,S^K_t) = 0 \tag{4.4.8}$$

with boundary condition

$$f(T,S^1_T,\ldots,S^K_T) = X\ , \tag{4.4.9}$$

then X is P^*-attainable. □

For special security price processes one can also show that condition (4.4.8) is necessary for P*-attainability under the conditions stated in Corollary 4.4.4. In particular, this applies to geometric Brownian motion. The corresponding equation is called *Kolmogorov's backward equation* in the literature. (Cf. GIHMAN/SKOROHOD (1972), pp. 73).

4.4.5 Example

Consider the security price process of Section 3.3.1. By means of Corollary 4.4.4 it will be shown that the contingent claim $X = (S_T^1 - K)^+$ is P*-attainable. By Example 4.1.8 the following holds true

$$X_t := E[X|F_t] = S_t^1 \, \Phi\left(\frac{\ln \frac{S_t^1}{K} + \frac{\sigma^2}{2}(T-t)}{\sigma\sqrt{T-t}}\right) - K\,\Phi\left(\frac{\ln \frac{S_t^1}{K} - \frac{\sigma^2}{2}(T-t)}{\sigma\sqrt{T-t}}\right).$$

In what follows we will use the notation introduced in Example 4.1.8. The function $f : [0,T] \times \mathbb{R} \to \mathbb{R}$ defined by

$$f(t,x) := x\,\Phi(g(t,x)) - K\,\Phi(h(t,x))$$

is twice continuously differentiable. In order to apply Corollary 4.4.4, the partial derivatives of f have to be determined. Using (4.1.16) we get

$$\frac{\partial f}{\partial S^1} = \Phi(g) + S^1 \frac{n(g)}{S^1 \sigma\sqrt{T-t}} - K \frac{n(h)}{S^1 \sigma\sqrt{T-t}} \tag{4.4.10}$$

$$= \Phi\left(\frac{\ln \frac{S_t^1}{K} + \frac{\sigma^2}{2}(T-t)}{\sigma\sqrt{T-t}}\right).$$

Thus (4.4.2) is given. Furthermore,

$$\frac{\partial^2 f}{(\partial S^1)^2} = \frac{n(g)}{S^1 \sigma\sqrt{T-t}} \tag{4.4.11}$$

$$\frac{\partial f}{\partial t} = S^1 \frac{hn(g)}{2(T-t)} - K \frac{gn(h)}{2(T-t)} \qquad (4.4.12)$$

$$= \frac{S^1 n(g)}{2(T-t)} (h - g)$$

$$= - \frac{\sigma S^1 n(g)}{2\sqrt{T-t}}$$

$[S^1 - S^1_o, S^1 - S^1_o]_t = \int\limits_0^t \sigma^2 (S^1)^2 ds$ implies (4.4.8). □

Remark

Corollary 4.4.4 deals with the classical arbitrage pricing of contingent claims due to BLACK/SCHOLES (1973) and MERTON (1973). The starting point is a functional relationship between the unknown price process of the contingent claim and the given security price process. Under suitable regularity conditions one derives the stochastic differential of the unknown price process. Choosing a suitable trading strategy this stochastic differential reduces to a partial differential or a difference-differential equation. The solution to this equation with the corresponding boundary condition is the pricing formula, one was looking for. Of course, this method has to be criticized on the grounds that it provides a solution to the valuation problem of a contingent claim only within the class of C^2 functions of the underlying stock price process and time.

4.5 Complete securities market models

This section considers securities market models, in which every contingent claim is P^*-attainable. These models are of special importance, since every contingent claim has a preference-free valuation given by its expected value.

4.5.1 Definition

A continuous-time securities market model is called P^*-*complete* if and only if every contingent claim is P^*-attainable.

Examples of P^*-complete securities market models have already been given. Section 4.3.1 shows that the securities market model based on a geometric Brownian motion security price process is P-complete. A similar result has been obtained in Section 4.3.3 for a geometric Poisson process. In both cases the set of equivalent martingale measures turned out to be singleton. The following theorem shows that P^*-complete securities market models are characterized by a similar property.

4.5.2 Theorem

A securities market model is P^*-complete if and only if $\mathbb{Q}(S) = \{P^*\}$ holds true.

Proof:

If $\mathbb{Q}(S) = \{P^*\}$, Theorem 4.2.4 implies the P^*-attainability of every contingent claim. Now suppose the securities market model considered is P^*-complete, i.e. every contingent claim X is P^*-attainable. This implies

$$\mathcal{L}(P^*) = \mathcal{H}^2(P^*) \text{ and } (\mathcal{L}(P^*))^\perp = \{0\}.$$

Since

$$\{N \mid N := M-1,\ M = (E^*[M_T \mid \mathcal{F}_t])_{t\in[0,T]},\ M_T := \frac{dQ}{dP^*},\ Q \in \mathbb{Q}(S)\}$$

is a subset of $(\mathcal{L}(P^*))^\perp$, $\mathbb{Q}(S) = \{P^*\}$ holds true. □

Remark

Because of Theorem 4.5.2 we speak of *complete securities market models* instead of P^*- complete securities market models.

An immediate consequence of Theorem 4.5.2 can be found in the following corollary.

4.5.3 Corollary

Suppose the securities market model fulfills (4.2.4) or (4.2.5). Then the securities market model is complete if and only if $\mathbb{P}(S) = \{P^*\}$ holds true.

Remarks

1. A further sufficient condition for completeness can be given, which is based on a set $\mathbb{P}_{loc}(S)$ of *local equivalent martingale measures*. The attributive "local" refers to the local martingale property of the underlying security price process S with respect to the elements of $\mathbb{P}_{loc}(S)$. The elements of $\mathbb{P}_{loc}(S)$ are probability measures that are equivalent to P. Then $|\mathbb{P}_{loc}(S)| = 1$ implies the completeness of the model. By defining a class of trading strategies that fulfill the integrability condition for the existence of the stochastic integral only locally, the equivalence of completeness and $|\mathbb{P}_{loc}(S)| = 1$ can be shown. The derivation of these results is rather technical. That is why those generalizations are dispensed with. As to the mathematical techniques to employ we refer to DELLACHERIE/MEYER (1982), Chapter VII, VIII, JACOD (1979), Chapter XI and ELLIOTT (1982), Chapters 10 - 12.
2. HARRISON/PLISKA (cf. HARRISON/PLISKA (1981) p. 241, HARRISON/PLISKA (1983), p. 314) claim that the set of equivalent L^1 martingale measures being singleton is a sufficient condition for completeness, without assuming that the components of the process $S - S_o$ are strongly orthogonal. Without the orthogonality assumption, this statement is not true as can be shown by means of Example 4.6.3 given below.

4.6 Counterexamples

In this section it will be shown by means of examples that the results of Chapter 4 are no longer true without the assumptions given there.

First of all, the question is addressed, whether the introduction of a continuous-time trading model is necessary indeed for valuation purposes. It will be shown that there are P^*-attainable contingent claims that are not simply attainable.

4.6.1 Example

We consider the securities market model introduced in Section 3.3.1. In Section 4.3.1 it is shown that every contingent claim is P-attainable in this model. In particular this applies to the contingent claim W_T, where $(W_t)_{t\in[0,T]}$ denotes the Brownian motion given. Suppose W_T is simply attainable, i.e. there exists a simple selffinancing trading strategy $\phi \in \Phi_0$ such that

$$W_T = \phi_T^0 + \phi_T^1 S_T^1 \qquad \text{P a.s.}$$

holds true. By Lemma 4.1.2 the associated value process $V(\phi)$ is a martingale with respect to P. For all $t \in [0,T]$ we obtain

$$W_t = E[W_T | F_t] = \phi_t^0 + \phi_t^1 S_t^1 \qquad \text{P a.s.} \tag{4.6.1}$$

The value of the portfolio held according to strategy ϕ is given by $\phi_0^0 + \phi_0^1 S_t^1$ between time 0 and the first trading date t_1 after 0. By assumption, ϕ_0^0 and ϕ_0^1 are F_0 - measurable, where F_0 is given by $F_0 = A(\{F \in F | P(F) = 0\})$. Thus ϕ_0^0 and ϕ_0^1 are constant P a.s. If $\phi_0^1 = 0$, (4.6.1) gives the contradiction

$$W_t = \phi_0^0 = \text{constant} \qquad t \in (0,t_1) \qquad \text{P a.s.}$$

Therefore consider $\phi_0^1 \neq 0$. (4.6.1) implies

$$\frac{W_t - \phi_0^0}{\phi_0^1} = S_t^1 \qquad \text{P a.s.} \tag{4.6.2}$$

(4.6.2) gives the following contradiction. The right-hand side of (4.6.2) represents a lognormal distributed random variable, whereas the left-hand side of (4.6.2) is normally distributed with mean $-\frac{\phi_0^0}{\phi_0^1}$ and variance $\frac{1}{(\phi_0^1)^2}\, t$.

Now we consider a securities market model that does not fulfill assumption (3.1.3).

4.6.2 Example

In Example 4.1.8 it is shown that the contingent claim $X = (S_T^1 - K)^+$ is P-attainable in the securities market model associated with a geometric Brownian motion stock price process. Now consider a Brownian motion W and an independent random variable 1_A on a probability space (Ω, F, P^*) with $P^*(A) = \theta^*$, $\theta^* \in (0,1)$. As to the existence of such a probability space we refer to Section 3.3.2. A filtration is described by

$$F_t = A(\{W_s | s \leq t\} \cup \{1_A\}) \qquad \forall t \in [0,T] ,$$

which is assumed to fulfill the usual conditions, and a security price process S^1 is given by

$$S_t^1 = S_o^1 \, 1_A \exp(\sigma_1 W_t - \frac{\sigma_1^2}{2} t) + S_o^1 \, 1_{A^c} \exp(\sigma_2 W_t - \frac{\sigma_2^2}{2} t) . \qquad (4.6.3)$$

σ_1, σ_2 and S_o^1 denote positive real numbers with $\sigma_1 \neq \sigma_2$. (4.6.3) describes a security price process that evolves like a geometric Brownian motion depending on the outcome of an event at t = 0. It will be shown that the contingent claim $X = (S_T^1 - K)^+$ is not P^*-attainable. This will be done as in Section 4.3.2. For $\theta \in (0,1)$, f_θ is defined by

$$f_\theta(\omega) := \frac{\theta}{\theta^*} 1_A(\omega) + \frac{1-\theta}{1-\theta^*} 1_{A^c}(\omega) .$$

f_θ is the Radon-Nikodym derivative of a probability measure P_θ with respect to P^*. Obviously, $P_\theta \in \mathbb{P}(S)$. We determine the expected value of $(S_T^1 - K)^+$ with respect to the equivalent martingale measures P_θ. Similar to 4.3.2 we get

$$E_\theta[(S_T^1 - K)^+] = \theta\left(S_o^1\,\Phi\left(\frac{\ln\frac{S_o^1}{K} + \frac{\sigma_1^2}{2}T}{\sigma_1\sqrt{T}}\right) - K\,\Phi\left(\frac{\ln\frac{S_o^1}{K} - \frac{\sigma_1^2}{2}T}{\sigma_1\sqrt{T}}\right)\right)$$

$$+ (1-\theta)\left(S_o^1\,\Phi\left(\frac{\ln\frac{S_o^1}{K} + \frac{\sigma_2^2}{2}T}{\sigma_2\sqrt{T}}\right) - K\,\Phi\left(\frac{\ln\frac{S_o^1}{K} - \frac{\sigma_2^2}{2}T}{\sigma_2\sqrt{T}}\right)\right)$$

$E_\theta[(S_T^1 - K)^+]$ is constant for all P_θ, $\theta \in (0,1)$, if and only if $f(K) = 0$ holds true, where $f(K)$ is defined by

$$f(K) := S_o^1\,\Phi\left(\frac{\ln\frac{S_o^1}{K} + \frac{\sigma_1^2}{2}T}{\sigma_1\sqrt{T}}\right) - K\,\Phi\left(\frac{\ln\frac{S_o^1}{K} - \frac{\sigma_1^2}{2}T}{\sigma_1\sqrt{T}}\right)$$

$$- S_o^1\,\Phi\left(\frac{\ln\frac{S_o^1}{K} + \frac{\sigma_2^2}{2}T}{\sigma_2\sqrt{T}}\right) + K\,\Phi\left(\frac{\ln\frac{S_o^1}{K} - \frac{\sigma_2^2}{2}T}{\sigma_2\sqrt{T}}\right)$$

As in Section 4.3.2 this can be shown to be equivalent to $\sigma_1 = \sigma_2$. Thus X is not P^*-attainable.

Without the strong orthogonality assumption (4.1.3) Theorem 4.2.4 is no longer true. This will be shown by means of the following example. This example is closely related to an example given by JACOD/YOR (1977), p. 87.

4.6.3 Example

Let W be a two-dimensional Brownian motion with independent components W^1 and W^2 on a probability space $(\Omega, \mathcal{F}, P)$. Let $\mathbb{F}$ be the filtration generated by W. We consider a predictable process u with values in (0,1), i.e. $0 < u_t < 1 \quad \forall t \in [0,T] \quad P$ a.s. Three security price processes are described by

$$S_t^o := 1 \qquad \forall t \in [0,T]$$

$$S_t^1 := S_o^1 \exp\left(W_t^1 - \tfrac{1}{2}t\right) \qquad \forall t \in [0,T]$$

$$S_t^2 := S_o^2 \exp\left(R_t - \frac{1}{2}[R,R]_t\right) \qquad \forall t \in [0,T]$$

for positive real numbers S_o^1 , S_o^2, where R is defined by

$$R := \int u dW^1 + \int (1 - u) dW^2 .$$

Let $E[\int \exp(2R)(u^2+(1-u)^2)\, dt] < \infty$. S^1 and S^2 are square-integrable martingales with respect to P. Consider $Q \in \mathbb{Q}(S^1,S^2)$. Then Q = P holds true, i.e. there exists only one P-continuous signed martingale measure. This can be seen by the following argument. First of all, note that $L(S^o,W^1,W^2) = H^2(P)$ holds true (cf. ELLIOTT(1982), p. 146, 12.34). Let K denote the following set

$$K := \{\phi_o^o + \int\phi^1 dS^1 + \int\phi^2 dS^2 \mid \phi_o^o \in \mathbb{R},\ \phi^k \text{ predictable},$$
$$E[\int_o^T (\phi^k)^2\, d[S^k,S^k]] < \infty \ ,\ k=1,2\} \tag{4.6.4}$$

By JACOD (1979), p. 116, (4.7),Q is a martingale measure for every element of $\bar{K}$, the closure of K in $H^2(P)$. Using the exponential formula it can be shown as in 4.3.1 that W^1 and R are elements of K. Thus $V := \int(1 - u)\, dW^2$ is an element of K, since it is the difference of R and $\int u dW^1$. Since u only takes values in (0,1) there is an increasing sequence $(A_n)_{n\in\mathbb{N}}$ of predictable sets defined by

$$A_n := \{(t,\omega) \mid \frac{1}{1-u(t,\omega)} \leqq n\}$$

We get

$$\bigcup_{n\in\mathbb{N}} A_n = [0,T] \times \Omega$$

and

$$V_n := \int 1_{A_n} \frac{1}{1-u}\, dV$$

defines a sequence of elements of K. We obtain

$$V_n = \int 1_{A_n}\, dW^2$$

and using Lebesgue's theorem this implies

$$V_n \overset{H^2(P)}{\rightarrow} W^2$$

Thus Q is a P-continuous, signed martingale measure with respect to W^1 and W^2, i.e. $Q \in \mathfrak{Q}(S^o,W^1,W^2)$. Let M_T denote the Radon-Nikodym derivative of Q with respect to P and M the P-martingale $M := (E[M_T|F_t])_{t\in[0,T]}$. $Q \in \mathfrak{Q}(S^o,W^1,W^2)$ implies

$$N := M - 1 \in (L(S^o,W^1,W^2))^{\perp}.$$

Thus N is identical to zero, since $(L(S^o,W^1,W^2))^{\perp} = \{0\}$ holds true. Now we assume that every contingent claim X is P-attainable. In particular, this applies to the contingent claim $X = W_T^2$.

Since $K \subset L(S^o,W^1,W^2)$, there exist predictable v and w fulfilling

$$E^*[\int_0^T v^2 d[W^1,W^1]] < \infty$$

$$E^*[\int_0^T w^2 d[R,R]] < \infty$$

such that

$$W^2 = \int v \, dW^1 + \int w \, dR \tag{4.6.5}$$

holds true. Thus we get a decomposition of W^2 into an element of $L(W^1)$ and $(L(W^1))^{\perp}$, i.e.

$$W^2 = \int (v + wu) \, dW^1 + \int w(1-u) \, dW^2 \quad .$$

Since this decomposition is unique, this implies

$$\int (v + wu) \, dW^1 = 0$$

and

$$\int w(1-u) \, dW^2 = W^2$$

which yields

$$\int_0^t (v + wu)^2 ds = 0 \qquad \forall\, t \in [0,T]$$

$$\int_0^t w^2 (1-u)^2 ds = t \qquad \forall\, t \in [0,T]$$

Thus necessarily v and w are of the form $v = -\frac{u}{1-u}$ and $w = \frac{1}{1-u}$.

Choose u in the following way.

$$u_s = \begin{cases} 1 - s & 0 < s < 1 \\ \frac{1}{2} & s = 0,\ s \geq 1 \end{cases}$$

For $\varepsilon > 0$ we get

$$\begin{aligned} \int_0^1 v^2\, d[W^1,W^1] &= \int_0^1 v_s^2\, ds \\ &\geqq \int_\varepsilon^1 \frac{(1-s)^2}{s^2}\, ds \\ &\geqq \int_\varepsilon^1 \left(\frac{1}{s^2} - \frac{2}{s}\right) ds \\ &= -1 + \frac{1}{\varepsilon} + 2 \ln \varepsilon \\ &= -1 + \ln\left(\varepsilon^2 \exp\left(\frac{1}{\varepsilon}\right)\right) \\ &\geqq -1 + 1/6 \ln(1/\varepsilon) \end{aligned}$$

yielding $\int_0^1 v^2\, d[W^1,W^1] = \infty$. Thus X is not P^*-attainable for the set K for $T \leqq 1$. If $T > 1$ u has to be changed in an obvious way.

5 Extensions of the BLACK/SCHOLES Model

This chapter aims at deriving preference independent valuations of contingent claims in an extended BLACK/SCHOLES model. The question of completeness is addressed and selffinancing generating trading strategies are determined for specific contingent claims. Apart from valuation purposes the determination of selffinancing generating trading strategies might be of interest for the purpose of hedging.

BLACK/SCHOLES (1973) considered the problem of pricing a European call option on a stock with exercise price K and expiration date T in an economy with a riskless bond and the stock. In their model the prices of these securities are given by

$$S_t^o = S_o^o \exp(rt) \tag{5.0.1}$$

$$S_t^1 = S_o^1 \exp(\sigma W_t + (\mu - \frac{1}{2}\sigma^2)t) \tag{5.0.2}$$

for $t \in [0,T]$. S_o^o, S_o^1, r,μ and σ denote positive constants and $W = (W_t)_{t\in[0,T]}$ a standard Brownian motion. Besides the assumptions already introduced in Chapters 3 and 4, the BLACK/SCHOLES model allows only for uncertainty with respect to security prices, i.e. the information available at time t consists only of information on stock prices up to time t.

$$\mathcal{F}_t = \mathcal{A}(\{W_s \mid s \leq t\}) \tag{5.0.3}$$

(5.0.1) and (5.0.2) are often given in their stochastic differential form (cf. the Appendix) by

$$dS^o = rS^o\, dt \tag{5.0.4}$$

$$dS^1 = \sigma S^1\, dW + \mu S^1\, dt \tag{5.0.5}$$

Note that (5.0.5) is of the general form

$$dS^1 = \sigma(t,S^1)\, dW + \mu(t,S^1)\, dt\ , \tag{5.0.6}$$

where $\sigma(t,S^1)$ and $\mu(t,S^1)$ are defined by

$$\sigma(t,S^1) = \sigma S^1 \tag{5.0.7}$$

$$\mu(t,S^1) = \mu S^1 \tag{5.0.8}$$

The model that we consider consists of securities with price processes (5.0.4) and (5.0.6). We also discuss generalizations of the bond price process (5.0.4). In order to apply the theory developed in Chapter 4, a discounted price process $Z := (Z^o, Z^1)$ is defined by

$$Z_t^o = 1 \qquad \forall\ t \in [0,T]$$

$$Z_t^1 = \frac{S_t^1}{S_t^o} \qquad \forall\ t \in [0,T]$$

This chapter proceeds as follows. In Section 5.1 an equivalent martingale measure for the discounted price process Z is determined. Section 5.2 deals with the relationship between the original and the discounted model. Section 5.3 addresses the question of completeness and determines selffinancing generating trading strategies for specific contingent claims. Section 5.4 relaxes the assumptions of the BLACK/SCHOLES model while keeping its completeness. Section 5.5 shows which assumptions of the BLACK/SCHOLES model are indispensable for completeness and lists possible sources of incompleteness.

5.1 Determination of an equivalent martingale measure

In this section an equivalent martingale measure is determined for a price process S^1 of the form (5.0.6) with initial condition $S_o^1 \in \mathbb{R}_{++}$. First of all, however, suitable regularity conditions are introduced that guarantee the existence of a process S^1 with (5.0.6) (cf. GIHMAN/SKOROHOD (1972), Theorem 1, p. 40). This is done in the first part of the following theorem. The second part concerns the determination of an equivalent martingale measure, which is achieved by combining GIRSANOV's theorem (cf. ELLIOTT (1982), Corollary 13.25, p. 169) and a result of NOVIKOV (cf. ELLIOTT (1982), Theorem 13.27, p. 170).

5.1.1 Theorem[1)]

Let $\mu: [0,T] \times \mathbb{R} \to \mathbb{R}$, $\sigma: [0,T] \times \mathbb{R} \to \mathbb{R}_{++}$ be measurable with respect to all their arguments.

(a) If there is a constant C such that

$$|\mu(t,x)-\mu(t,y)|+|\sigma(t,x)-\sigma(t,y)| \leqq C|x - y| \tag{5.1.1}$$

$$|\mu(t,x)|^2+|\sigma(t,x)|^2 \leqq C^2(1 + x^2) \tag{5.1.2}$$

holds true for all $t \in [0,T]$ and all $x,y \in \mathbb{R}$, there exists a unique, continuous, square integrable process S^1 that fulfills (5.0.6)

(b) Furthermore, if $\mu(.,S^1)$, $\sigma(.,S^1)$ are predictable and cadlag, and

$$\int_0^T \frac{\mu^2(t,S^1)}{\sigma^2(t,S^1)} dt < \infty \qquad P \text{ a.s.} \tag{5.1.3}$$

and

$$E[\exp(\frac{1}{2}\int_0^T \frac{\mu^2(t,S^1)}{\sigma^2(t,S^1)} dt)] < \infty \tag{5.1.4}$$

holds true,

$$f_T := \exp(-\int_0^T \frac{\mu(t,S^1)}{\sigma(t,S^1)} dW_t - \frac{1}{2}\int_0^T \frac{\mu^2(t,S^1)}{\sigma^2(t,S^1)} dt) \tag{5.1.5}$$

is the Radon-Nikodym derivative of a probability measure P^* which is equivalent to P with the property that

$$W_t^* := W_t + \int_0^t \frac{\mu(s,S^1)}{\sigma(s,S^1)} ds \tag{5.1.6}$$

---

1) See also HARRISON/KREPS (1979), pp. 394

is a standard Brownian motion with respect to P^*. If $E[f_T^2] < \infty$ and $E^*[\int_0^T \sigma^2(t,S^1)\,dt] < \infty$, P^* is an equivalent martingale measure and $\mathbb{Q}(S^1) = \mathbb{P}(S^1) = \{P^*\}$.

5.1.2 Example

The discounted process

$$Z_t^1 := Z_0^1 \exp(\sigma W_t + (\mu - r - \tfrac{1}{2}\sigma^2)t)$$

associated with (5.0.1) and (5.0.2) fulfills the assumptions of Theorem 5.1.1. Thus we get

$$\mathbb{Q}(Z^1) = \mathbb{P}(Z^1) = \{P^*\} \quad ,$$

where P^* is defined by

$$dP^* = f_T\, dP \qquad \text{with}$$

$$f_T := \exp\left(- \frac{\mu - r}{\sigma} W_T - \frac{1}{2} \frac{(\mu - r)^2}{\sigma^2} T \right)$$

The discounted security price process Z^1 can be written in the form

$$Z_t^1 = Z_0^1 \exp(\sigma W_t^* - \tfrac{1}{2}\sigma^2 t).$$

Note that the equivalent martingale measure eliminates the drift term.[1)] By Theorem 4.2.4 every contingent claim X is P^*-attainable. Consider the contingent claim $\tilde{X}$ that represents the discounted value at T of a European call option on a stock with price process (5.0.2), exercise price K and expiration date T.

---

1) $\mu(t,S^1)$ of (5.0.6) is called the *drift*. (cf. GIHMAN/SKOROHOD (1972), p. 65 and Theorem 2, p. 68)

$$\tilde{X} := \frac{1}{S_T^o} \quad (S_T^1 - K)^+ \quad . \tag{5.1.7}$$

Since

$$\tilde{X} = (Z_T^1 - \frac{K}{S_o^o} \exp(-rT))^+ \quad , \tag{5.1.8}$$

$\tilde{X}$ is P^*-attainable in the discounted model. In Example 4.1.8 the selffinancing generating trading strategy is determined as

$$\phi_t^o = - \frac{K}{S_o^o} \exp(-rT) \ \Phi \ (\frac{\ln \frac{Z_t^1 \ S_o^o}{K \exp(-rT)} - \frac{\sigma^2}{2} \ (T-t)}{\sigma \sqrt{T-t}}) \tag{5.1.9}$$

$$= - \frac{K}{S_o^o} \exp(-rT) \ \Phi \ (\frac{\ln \frac{S_t^1}{K} + (r - \frac{\sigma^2}{2}) \ (T-t)}{\sigma \sqrt{T-t}})$$

$$\phi_t^1 = \Phi \ (\frac{\ln \frac{Z_t^1 \ S_o^o}{K \exp(-rT)} + \frac{\sigma^2}{2} \ (T-t)}{\sigma \sqrt{T-t}}) \tag{5.1.10}$$

$$= \Phi \ (\frac{\ln \frac{S_t^1}{K} + (r + \frac{\sigma^2}{2}) \ (T-t)}{\sigma \sqrt{T-t}})$$

for $t \in [0,T]$. □

Remark

It is easily seen that the trading strategy ϕ given in (5.1.9) and (5.1.10) generates the contingent claim $(S_T^1-K)^+$ in the original model, i.e.

$$\phi_T^o \ S_T^o + \phi_T^1 \ S_T^1 \quad = \quad (S_T^1-K)^+ \qquad P \text{ a.s.}$$

The corresponding portfolio value process in the original model, $V(\phi)= \phi S$, gives the BLACK/SCHOLES formula (cf. p.11).

5.2 The relationship between the original and the discounted model

Up to now all definitions and concepts are available only in the case that the bond's price process is given by (3.1.5). In the first part of this section the effects of a relaxation of this assumption are examined. These considerations provide the framework for the analysis of the extended BLACK/SCHOLES model.

We assume that the bond's price process is described by an arbitrary positive stochastic process, which is adapted to the information structure and has paths that are right continuous with left limits. We construct a new securities market model with the same probability space (Ω,F,P), set of trading dates $[0,T]$, information structure $(F_t)_{t\in[0,T]}$, but with price process $Z := (Z^0,Z^1,\dots,Z^K)$ defined by

$$Z_t^k = \frac{S_t^k}{S_t^0} \quad , \quad k \in \{0,\dots,K\} \; , \qquad \forall\, t \in [0,T] \; .$$

This model is called the *discounted continuous-time securities market model*, which is assumed to be viable, i.e. there exists $P^* \in \mathbb{P}(Z)$. We examine the relationship between P^*- attainable contingent claims and their associated contingent claims in the original model. In order to do this we assume that

$$S^0 \text{ and } (S^0)^{-1} \text{ are semimartingales} \tag{5.2.1}$$

and consider the subset of Φ_{P^*} given by

$$\Phi_{sm} := \{\, \phi = (\phi^0,\dots,\phi^K) \mid \phi^k \text{ predictable, cadlag,}$$
$$E^*\,[\int_0^T (\phi^k)^2 \, d[Z^k,Z^k]] < \infty,\ k \in \{0,\dots,K\}\}$$

Note that for $\phi \in \Phi_{sm}$, ϕ^k, $k \in \{0,\dots,K\}$, is locally bounded (cf. DELLACHERIE/MEYER(1982), p. 221). Thus the stochastic integral $\int \phi^k\, dS^k$, $k \in \{0,\dots,K\}$, is defined and it is a semimartingale (cf. JACOD(1979), pp 46). Now consider a selffinancing trading strategy $\phi \in \Phi_{sm}$ in the discounted model, i.e.

$$\phi^0 + \sum_{k=1}^{K} \phi^k z^k = \phi_0^0 + \sum_{k=1}^{K} \int \phi_s^k \, dz_s^k \qquad (5.2.2)$$

The following lemma shows that the value process in the original model associated with ϕ has a similar integral representation.

5.2.1 Lemma

(5.2.2) is equivalent to

$$\sum_{k=0}^{K} \phi^k \; S^k = \sum_{k=0}^{K} \int \phi_s^k \, dS_s^k \qquad (5.2.3)$$

Proof

Suppose that (5.2.2) holds true. First of all, Ito's lemma applied to products of semimartingales (cf. the Appendix) yields

$$\sum_{k=0}^{K} \phi^k S^k = S^0 \left(\sum_{k=0}^{K} \phi^k z^k \right)$$

$$= \int S_-^0 \, d\left(\sum_{k=0}^{K} \phi^k z^k \right) + \int \left(\sum_{k=0}^{K} \phi^k z^k \right)_- dS^0$$

$$+ \left[S^0, \sum_{k=0}^{K} \phi^k z^k \right] \qquad (5.2.4)$$

The terms in (5.2.4) can be simplified as follows.
Using the fact that

$$\Delta\left(\int \phi^k dz^k\right)_t = \phi_t^k \, \Delta z_t^k$$

holds true (cf. DELLACHERIE/MEYER(1982),p. 339, Theorem 30), we get

$$(\sum_{k=0}^{K} \phi^k z^k)_{t-} = (\sum_{k=0}^{K} \phi^k z^k)_t - \Delta(\sum_{k=0}^{K} \phi^k z^k)_t$$

$$= (\sum_{k=0}^{K} \phi^k z^k)_t - \sum_{k=0}^{K} \phi_t^k \Delta z_t^k$$

$$= \sum_{k=0}^{K} \phi_t^k z_{t-}^k \qquad (5.2.5)$$

Since

$$[S^0, \int \phi^k dz^k] = \int \phi^k \, d[S^0, z^k] \qquad k \in \{1,\dots,K\}$$

holds true for locally bounded integrands ϕ^k (cf. JACOD(1979),p. 47, Proposition (2.51)), the quadratic variation of S^0 and $\sum_{k=0}^{K} \phi^k z^k$ is given by

$$[S^0, \sum_{k=0}^{K} \phi^k z^k] = \sum_{k=0}^{K} \int \phi^k \, d[S^0, z^k] \qquad (5.2.6)$$

Then (5.2.4), (5.2.5) and (5.2.6) imply

$$\sum_{k=0}^{K} \phi^k S^k = \sum_{k=0}^{K} \int S_-^0 \phi^k dz^k + \sum_{k=0}^{K} \int \phi^k z_-^k \, dS^0 + \sum_{k=0}^{K} \int \phi^k \, d[S^0, z^k]$$ 1)

$$= \sum_{k=0}^{K} \Big(\int \phi^k S_-^0 \, d(S^k (S^0)^{-1}) + \int \phi^k (S^k (S^0)^{-1})_- dS^0$$

$$+ \int \phi^k d[S^0, S^k (S^0)^{-1}] \Big)$$

$$= \sum_{k=0}^{K} \int \phi^k dS^k$$

---

1) Note that S_-^0 is locally bounded, since it is a leftcontinuous, adapted process (cf. DELLACHERIE/MEYER (1982),p. 320,8)

Suppose that (5.2.3) holds true. Ito's Lemma applied to products of semimartingales and

$$\left(\sum_{k=0}^{K} \phi^k S^k\right)_- = \sum_{k=0}^{K} \phi^k S^k_- \tag{5.2.7}$$

$$\left[(S^0)^{-1}, \sum_{k=0}^{K} \phi^k S^k\right] = \sum_{k=0}^{K} \int \phi^k \, d[(S^0)^{-1}, S^k] \quad , \tag{5.2.8}$$

which is obtained similar to (5.2.5) and (5.2.6), yields

$$\sum_{k=0}^{K} \phi^k Z^k = (S^0)^{-1} \left(\sum_{k=0}^{K} \phi^k S^k\right)$$

$$= \int ((S^0)^{-1})_- d\left(\sum_{k=0}^{K} \phi^k S^k\right) + \int \left(\sum_{k=0}^{K} \phi^k S^k\right)_- d((S^0)^{-1})$$

$$+ \left[(S^0)^{-1}, \sum_{k=0}^{K} \phi^k S^k\right]$$

$$= \sum_{k=0}^{K} \left(\int \phi^k ((S^0)^{-1})_- dS^k + \int \phi^k S^k_- d((S^0)^{-1}) \right.$$

$$\left. + \int \phi^k d[(S^0)^{-1}, S^k] \right)$$

$$= \sum_{k=0}^{K} \int \phi^k dZ^k \quad \square$$

<u>Remarks</u>

1. Lemma 5.2.1 extends a result of HARRISON/PLISKA(1981). Proposition 3.24 of HARRISON/PLISKA(1981) states the equivalence of (5.2.2) and (5.2.3) for trading strategies ϕ with locally bounded and predictable components ϕ^k, $k \in \{0,\dots K\}$ in the case that S^0 is a continuous process of finite variation. The proof of Lemma 5.2.1 shows that this statement is true for more general bond processes S^0. It

might seem that Proposition 3.24 is slightly more general in that the semimartingale property of $(S^0)^{-1}$ is not assumed. In the proof of Proposition 3.24, however, HARRISON/PLISKA make use of the properties that $(S^0)^{-1}$ is continuous and of finite variation. Thus, in particular, $(S^0)^{-1}$ is a semimartingale. Those properties used by HARRISON/PLISKA do not follow from the corresponding assumption on S^0: they have to be guaranteed otherwise. A sufficient condition for the equivalence to be true would be the existence of a random variable L such that

$$S^0(t,\omega) \geqq L(\omega) > 0 \qquad \forall\, t \in [0,T] \qquad P \text{ a.s.}$$

holds true.

2. Without the semimartingale assumption on $(S^0)^{-1}$, Lemma 5.2.1 is no longer true. A counterexample can easily be constructed.

Let $\tilde{X}$ be a P*- attainable contingent claim in the discounted securities market model with associated generating trading strategy $\phi \in \Phi_{sm}$. Then $X = S_T^0\,\tilde{X}$ is a contingent claim in the original model such that

$$X = \sum_{k=0}^{K} \phi_T^k S_T^k \tag{5.2.9}$$

$$\sum_{k=0}^{K} \phi^k S^k = \sum_{k=0}^{K} \int \phi^k \, dS^k \tag{5.2.10}$$

holds true. A contingent claim X that fulfills (5.2.9) and (5.2.10) for a trading strategy $\phi \in \Phi_{sm}$ is called *P*- attainable in the original model.*

5.2.2 Example

S^0 of the form (5.0.1) satisfies the assumption (5.2.1). By Lemma 5.2.1 the contingent claim $(S_T^1 - K)^+$ is P - attainable in the continuous-time securities market model with price processes of the form (5.0.1) and (5.0.2). Its generating trading strategy is given by (5.1.8) and (5.1.9), i.e.

$$(S_T^1 - K)^+ = \phi_T^0 S_T^0 + \phi_T^1 S_T^1$$

$$\phi^0 S^0 + \phi^1 S^1 = \int \phi^0 \, dS^0 + \int \phi^1 \, dS^1 .$$

5.3 Completeness and the determination of selffinancing trading strategies in the case of a European call option

In this section continuous-time securities market models are discussed, where the basic discounted security price process is of the form

$$dZ^1 = \sigma(t,Z^1)dW + \mu(t,Z^1)dt \tag{5.3.1}$$

with

$$\sigma(t,Z^1) = \sigma(t)Z^1 \tag{5.3.2}$$

Models of this kind are quite popular in the literature on contingent claim valuation. The question of completeness is addressed. Furthermore, for different processes σ selffinancing trading strategies are determined that generate the contingent claim $(Z_T^1 - K)^+$ representing the discounted value at T of a European call option.

In order to determine generating selffinancing trading strategies two different methods may be chosen in principle. The first method is outlined in Example 4.1.8. It is based on the determination of the conditional expectation $E^*[X|F_t]$ of the given contingent claim X. It is hoped for that the conditional expectation will explicitly give generating trading strategies. Having obtained a generating trading strategy this way, it remains to check, whether it is self-financing, i.e. whether $V(\phi)$ equals $\int\phi dS$. The second method is based on the relationship (4.4.1). It aims at simultaneously determining the function f and the generating self-financing trading strategy. Under suitable regularity conditions one derives the stochastic differential of the unknown price process. Choosing a suitable trading strategy, this stochastic differential reduces to a partial differential equation or a difference-differential equation. The solution to this equation is the pricing formula, one was looking for. Having obtained this solution the generating trading strategy can be given explicitly. The conditions derived in Section 4.4 may be used in actually showing that the generating trading strategy is selffinancing. In this section, however, we choose the approach of Example 4.1.8.

5.3.1 Example

Let $\mu:[0,T] \to \mathbb{R}_{++}$ be bounded and left-continuous. For $t_i \in [0,T]$, $i = 0,\dots,N$, $N \in \mathbb{N}$, such that $0 = t_0 < t_1 < \dots < t_N = T$, and positive numbers σ_i, $i = 0,\dots,N-1$, a variance process σ is defined by

$$\sigma(t) = \sigma_0 1_{\{0\}}(t) + \sum_{i=1}^{N} \sigma_{i-1} 1_{(t_{i-1},t_i]}(t) \quad {}^{1)} . \qquad (5.3.3)$$

By GIHMAN/SKOROHOD(1972), Example 3, p. 36, the solution of

$$dZ^1 = \sigma(t) Z^1 dW^*$$

with initial condition $Z_0^1 > 0$ is given by

$$Z_t^1 = Z_0^1 \exp\left(\int_0^t \sigma(s) dW_s^* - \frac{1}{2} \int_0^t \sigma^2(s) ds \right) \qquad \forall\, t \in [0,T], (5.3.4)$$

which can be simplified yielding

$$Z_t^1 = Z_0^1 \exp\{ \sum_{i=1}^{N} (\sigma_{i-1}(W^*_{t_i \wedge t} - W^*_{t_{i-1} \wedge t})$$

$$- \frac{1}{2} \sigma_{i-1}^2 (t_i \wedge t - t_{i-1} \wedge t))\} \qquad (5.3.5)$$

1) There is no gain in generality if one assumes σ to be of the form (3.1.9), since $\int \sigma(s) dW_s^*$ is considered, which always yields $\sigma(0) W_0^* = 0$ P^* a.s. independent of the initial value of the process σ.

By Theorem 5.1.1 this securities market model is complete. As in Example 4.1.8 we determine a selffinancing trading strategy that generates the contingent claim $(Z_T^1 - K)^+$. We use the following notation. For $t \in [0,T]$ we define a random variable Y_t and a real number $\sigma^*(t)$ by

$$Y_t := \int_t^T \sigma(s)\,dW_s^* - \frac{1}{2}\int_t^T \sigma^2(s)\,ds \tag{5.3.6}$$

$$\sigma^*(t) := \int_t^T \sigma^2(s)\,ds \quad . \tag{5.3.7}$$

Note that Y_t is normally distributed with mean $-\frac{1}{2}\sigma^*(t)$ and variance $\sigma^*(t)$. Furthermore, Y_t is independent of Z_t^1. Using the Markov property and the stochastic independence of the increments of Brownian motion as well as (4.1.12) and (4.1.13) we get

$$\begin{aligned} E^*[(Z_T^1 - K)^+ | F_t] &= Z_t^1\, E^*[\exp(Y_t)\, 1_{\{\exp(Y_t) > \frac{K}{Z_t^1}\}} | A(Z_t^1)] \\ &\quad - KE^*[1_{\{\exp(Y_t) > \frac{K}{Z_t^1}\}} | A(Z_t^1)] \\ &= Z_t^1\, \Phi\left(\frac{\ln \frac{Z_t^1}{K} + \frac{1}{2}\sigma^*(t)}{\sqrt{\sigma^*(t)}}\right) \\ &\quad - K\,\Phi\left(\frac{\ln \frac{Z_t^1}{K} - \frac{1}{2}\sigma^*(t)}{\sqrt{\sigma^*(t)}}\right) \end{aligned}$$

Thus

$$\phi_t^0 := -K\,\Phi\left(\frac{\ln \frac{Z_t^1}{K} - \frac{1}{2}\sigma^*(t)}{\sqrt{\sigma^*(t)}}\right) \tag{5.3.8}$$

$$\phi_t^1 := \Phi\left(\frac{\ln \frac{Z_t^1}{K} + \frac{1}{2}\sigma^*(t)}{\sqrt{\sigma^*(t)}}\right) \tag{5.3.9}$$

generates the contingent claim $(Z_T^1 - K)^+$.
ϕ^0 and ϕ^1 are predictable. It remains to show that this trading strategy is selffinancing. In doing this the following notation will be used.

$$g(t,Z^1) := \frac{\ln \frac{Z^1}{K} + \frac{1}{2}\sigma^*(t)}{\sqrt{\sigma^*(t)}} \tag{5.3.10}$$

$$h(t,Z^1) := \frac{\ln \frac{Z^1}{K} - \frac{1}{2}\sigma^*(t)}{\sqrt{\sigma^*(t)}} \tag{5.3.11}$$

Note that

$$h(t,Z^1) = g(t,Z^1) - (\sigma^*(t))^{1/2} \tag{5.3.12}$$

holds true. Furthermore, σ^* is a continuous process of finite variation, i.e. σ^* is a continuous semimartingale. By JACOD (1979),p. 48, g and h defined by (5.3.10) and (5.3.11) are continuous semimartingales. Since the semimartingale property is preserved under twice continuously differentiable functions, ϕ is a semimartingale, too. Thus we can apply Ito's lemma, which yields

$$\begin{aligned} V(\phi) &= \phi^0 + \int \phi^1_- \, dZ^1 + \int Z^1_- \, d\phi^1 + [\phi^1, Z^1] \\ &= \phi^0_0 + \int \phi^1 \, dZ^1 + (\phi^0 - \phi^0_0) + \int Z^1 \, d(\phi^1 - \phi^1_0) \\ &\quad + [\phi^1 - \phi^1_0, Z^1] \end{aligned}$$

It remains to show that

$$C := (\phi^0 - \phi^0_0) + \int Z^1 \, d(\phi^1 - \phi^1_0) + [\phi^1 - \phi^1_0, Z^1] \equiv 0 .$$

In what follows the notation introduced in Example 4.1.8 will be used. By Ito's lemma we get

$$\phi^0 - \phi^0_0 = -K \{ \int n(h)_- dh - \frac{1}{2} \int h_- n(h) d[h,h] \}$$

and

$$\phi^1 - \phi_0^1 = \int n(g)\_dg - \frac{1}{2} \int g\_n(g)d[g,g] .$$

C can be written in the form

$$C = -K \{ \int n(h)\_dh - \frac{1}{2} \int h\_n(h)\ d[h,h]\} + \int Z^1 n(g)\_dg$$

$$- \frac{1}{2} \int Z^1 g\_n(g)\ d[g,g] + \int n(g)\_d[g,Z^1] \qquad (5.3.13)$$

The various terms will be determined in several steps. We get by Ito's lemma (cf. JACOD(1979), Theorème (2.54),p. 48)

(i) $(\sigma^*)^{1/2} = \frac{1}{2} \int ((\sigma^*)^{-1/2})\_d\sigma^*$

(ii) $g = g(0,Z_0^1) + \int ((Z^1(\sigma^*)^{1/2})^{-1})\_dZ^1 - \int h\_(2\sigma^*)^{-1}d\sigma^*$

$$- \frac{1}{2} \int (((Z^1)^2(\sigma^*)^{1/2})^{-1})\_d[Z^1,Z^1]$$

We used the fact that for m and p defined by

$$m(x,y) := \frac{\ln x - \ln K + \frac{1}{2} y}{y^{1/2}}$$

$$p(x,y) := \frac{\ln x - \ln K - \frac{1}{2} y}{y^{1/2}}$$

$$\partial m/\partial x = (xy^{1/2})^{-1}$$

$$\partial^2 m/(\partial x)^2 = -(x^2 y^{1/2})^{-1}$$

$$\partial m/\partial y = -p(2y)^{-1}$$

holds true.

(iii) $h = h(0,Z_0^1) + \int ((Z^1(\sigma^*)^{1/2})^{-1})\_dZ^1 - \int g\_(2\sigma^*)^{-1}d\sigma^*$

$$- \frac{1}{2} \int (((Z^1)^2(\sigma^*)^{1/2})^{-1})\_d[Z^1,Z^1]$$

We used the fact that

$$\partial p/\partial x = (xy^{1/2})^{-1}$$

$$\partial^2 p/(\partial x)^2 = -(x^2y^{1/2})^{-1}$$

$$\partial p/\partial y = -m(2y)^{-1}$$

holds true.

Using the relationship

$$Kn(h) = Z^1 n(g) \tag{5.3.14}$$

the following calculation will show that ϕ is selffinancing.

$$C = -K \{ \int n(h)\_(Z^1(\sigma*)^{1/2})^{-1} dZ^1 - \frac{1}{2} \int n(h)\_g(\sigma*)^{-1} d\sigma*$$

$$- \frac{1}{2} \int n(h)\_((Z^1)^2(\sigma*)^{1/2})^{-1} \, d[Z^1,Z^1]$$

$$- \frac{1}{2} \int h\_n(h)\_((Z^1)^2\sigma*)^{-1} \, d[Z^1,Z^1]\}$$

$$+ \int Z^1 n(g)\_(Z^1(\sigma*)^{1/2})^{-1} \, dZ^1 - \frac{1}{2} \int Z^1 n(g)\_h(\sigma*)^{-1} d\sigma*$$

$$- \frac{1}{2} \int Z^1 n(g)\_((Z^1)^2(\sigma*)^{1/2})^{-1} \, d[Z^1,Z^1]$$

$$- \frac{1}{2} \int Z^1 g\_n(g)((Z^1)^2\sigma*)^{-1} \, d[Z^1,Z^1]$$

$$+ \int n(g)\_(Z^1(\sigma*)^{1/2})^{-1} \, d[Z^1,Z^1]$$

$$= \frac{1}{2} \int Z^1 n(g)_-(\sigma^*)^{-1/2}\, d\sigma^*$$

$$- \frac{1}{2} \int K n(h)_-((Z^1)^2(\sigma^*)^{1/2})^{-1}\, d[Z^1,Z^1]$$

$$+ \int n(g)_-(Z^1(\sigma^*)^{1/2})^{-1}\, d[Z^1,Z^1]$$

$$= \frac{1}{2} \int Z^1 n(g)_-(\sigma^*)^{-1/2}\, d\sigma^*$$

$$+ \frac{1}{2} \int Z^1 n(g)_-((Z^1)^2(\sigma^*)^{1/2})^{-1}\, d[Z^1,Z^1]$$

$$= - \frac{1}{2} \int Z^1 n(g)_-(\sigma^*)^{-1/2}\, \sigma^2\, dt$$

$$+ \frac{1}{2} \int Z^1 n(g)_-(\sigma^*)^{-1/2}\, \sigma^2\, dt$$

Remark

In proving that the trading strategy $\phi := (\phi^0,\phi^1)$ of the form (5.3.8) and (5.3.9) with (5.3.7) is selffinancing we did not exploit the specific form of σ^* and (5.3.5). We only made use of the fact that σ^* is continuous. Thus (5.3.8) and (5.3.9) is a selffinancing trading strategy in a securities market model with security price process of the form (5.3.4) for a general σ^* with

$$\sigma^*(t) := \int_t^T \sigma_s^2 ds \tag{5.3.15}$$

Note that both ϕ^0 and ϕ^1 are continuous.

One might be interested in comparing the valuation of a European call option in discounted securities market models with the same initial stock price Z_0^1 but with different variance processes. Consider a process of the form (5.3.2) with constant σ and a process of the form (5.3.2) for general σ. Define a function $f: \mathbb{R}_{++} \to \mathbb{R}$ by

$$f(k) := Z_0^1 \, \Phi \left(\frac{\ln \frac{Z_0^1}{K} + \frac{1}{2} k}{k^{1/2}} \right) - K \, \Phi \left(\frac{\ln \frac{Z_0^1}{K} - \frac{1}{2} k}{k^{1/2}} \right)$$

It is easily seen that

$$f'(k) = Z_0^1 \, n \left(\frac{\ln \frac{Z_0^1}{K} + \frac{1}{2} k}{k^{1/2}} \right) \frac{1}{2k^{1/2}} > 0$$

holds true. If $\sigma < \sigma^*(0)$ the value of a European call option written on a stock with price process (5.3.2) for a constant σ is smaller than the value of a European call option written on a stock with price process (5.3.2)

5.3.2 Example

Consider bounded leftcontinuous functions μ and σ from $[0,T]$ into $\mathbb{R}_+$ such that $\sigma(t) > 0$ and

$$\int_0^T \frac{\mu^2(t)}{\sigma^2(t)} \, dt < \infty$$

holds true. Then the process Z^1 defined by

$$Z_t^1 = Z_0^1 \exp\left(\int_0^t \sigma(s) dW_s^* - \frac{1}{2} \int_0^t \sigma^2(s) ds\right)$$

is a solution of

$$dZ^1 = \sigma(t) Z^1 dW^*$$

(cf. GIHMAN/SKOROHOD(1972), Example 3, p. 36). By Theorem 5.1.1 the model is complete. Example 5.3.1 shows that the trading strategy ϕ defined by

$$\phi_t^0 := -K \; \Phi \left(\frac{\ln \frac{Z_t^1}{K} - \frac{1}{2}\sigma^*(t)}{\sqrt{\sigma^*(t)}} \right)$$

$$\phi_t^1 := \Phi \left(\frac{\ln \frac{Z_t^1}{K} + \frac{1}{2}\sigma^*(t)}{\sqrt{\sigma^*(t)}} \right) \tag{5.3.16}$$

with

$$\sigma^*(t) := \int_t^T \sigma^2(s)ds$$

is selffinancing. It is easily seen that

$$\phi_T^0 + \phi_T^1 Z_T^1 = (Z_T^1 - K)^+ \quad \text{a.s.}$$

holds true, i.e. the selffinancing trading strategy ϕ generates the contingent claim $(Z_T^1 - K)^+$.

Remark

By the technique employed in Examples 5.3.1 and 5.3.2 it can be shown that the contingent claim associated with a European call option written on a stock, the price process of which is described by a diffusion, can be generated in a selffinancing way by a portfolio in the stock and a riskless asset.

It is possible to consider more complicated σ provided they preserve predictability. If this is the case, one always has to check the existence of a solution to (5.0.6) and the possibility of transition to an equivalent martingale measure.

A process of the form (5.3.1), (5.3.2) is a special case of a process (5.3.1) with

$$\sigma(t,Z^1) = \sigma(t)(Z^1)^\alpha \qquad , \; \alpha \in \mathbb{R}_{++} \tag{5.3.17}$$

A process fulfilling (5.3.1) and (5.3.17) is not economically meaningful if $\alpha=0$, since it might take negative values. To see this, consider the special case $\mu(t,Z^1) = \mu(t)$. Under suitable regularity conditions, its solution is given by

$$Z_t^1 = \int_0^t \sigma(s)\,dW_s + \int_0^t \mu(s)\,ds \qquad \forall\, t \in [0,T] .$$

$\alpha = 1$ is the case most often encountered in the literature. In this case the resulting price process Z^1 may conveniently be determined by the exponential formula (cf. the Appendix). It is also conceivable to allow for a randomness in (5.3.1) that goes beyond the one represented by Z^1. But this approach might lead to incomplete models (cf. Section 5.5 on this). The models based on a process with $\alpha \neq 1$ are much more complicated to deal with. This is based on the fact that the distribution of Z^1 cannot be written down explicitly. But in principle, if one assumes that a solution of (5.0.6) exists and the transition to the equivalent martingale measure can be guaranteed, the approach outlined above to determine selffinancing trading strategies can be carried out.

5.4 Completeness and the relaxation of assumptions

Up to now some generalizations of the classical BLACK/SCHOLES model have already been discussed. This section aims at giving a summary of possible relaxations of assumptions under which the completeness of the securities market model is maintained. The relaxations that are dealt with are characterized by the fact that the assumption (5.0.3) on the filtration considered is kept.

The classical BLACK/SCHOLES model considers the pricing of a European call option written on a stock with a constant exercise price K and expiration date T. The basic securities are given by (5.0.1) and (5.0.6), where r, $\sigma(t,S^1)/S^1$ and $\mu(t,S^1)/S^1$ are constants. Relaxations of those terms will now be discussed.

In Section 5.2 it has already been shown that under certain conditions it is possible to replace the bond price process

$$S_t^o = S_o^o \exp(rt)$$

by a semimartingale. One of those conditions is the semimartingale property of the process $(S^o)^{-1}$. Furthermore, if S^o is a semimartingale with respect to the filtration (5.0.3), the discounted securities market model is complete. The valuation formulas in the original model may be derived from the valuation formulas in the discounted securities market model as shown in Section 5.2.

In Section 5.3 it is no longer assumed that $\sigma(t,S^1)/S^1$ and $\mu(t,S^1)/S^1$ are constants. Instead, more general functional relationships are allowed for. If $\sigma(.,S^1)/S^1$ and $\mu(.,S^1)/S^1$ are predictable processes fulfilling certain integrability conditions, the completeness of the model is maintained. However, the existence of a process of the form (5.0.6) might be rather difficult to guarantee for complicated functional relationships. Furthermore, the transition to an equivalent martingale measure has to be accomplished.

It is possible to give up the assumption of a constant exercise price. Provided that the exercise price is F-measurable the contingent claim associated with the corresponding call option remains attainable. The resulting valuation formula, however, might not be given in closed form. But it is possible to derive certain inequalities for it.

5.5 Incompleteness caused by variations of assumptions

All variations of the assumptions of the classical BLACK/SCHOLES model that cause incompleteness have a common feature: they violate assumption (5.0.3). If assumption (5.0.3) is given up, this results in an incomplete securities market model. To see this consider $t \in [0,T]$ such that

$$A \in F_t \setminus A(\{W_s | s \leq t\})$$

with $P(A)>0$. Then the contingent claim 1_A is not attainable.

This argument has the following implications. If one of the terms r, $\sigma(t,S^1)/S^1$, $\mu(t,S^1)/S^1$ or K associated with the extended BLACK/SCHOLES model is dependent on 1_A, where $A \in F_t \setminus A(\{W_s | s \leq t\})$ with $P(A)>0$ for a $t \in [0,T]$, the contingent claim associated with a European call option written on a stock with price process (5.0.6) is not attainable.

6 From Preference-free to Preference-dependent Valuations of Contingent Claims: the Hedge Approach in Incomplete Models

This chapter deals with the hedge approach in incomplete securities markets. Contingent claims are considered that cannot be priced according to the preference-free approach introduced in Chapter 4, since there do not exist selffinancing trading strategies generating them. Section 4.3.2 shows that such a situation might occur fairly easily. If one considers the BLACK/SCHOLES model with the only exception that the variance of the underlying stock price process changes, say, according to the outcome of an election, the contingent claim associated with a European call option on this stock cannot be generated by a selffinancing trading strategy in the bond and the stock. Thus a European call option on this stock cannot be priced uniquely by the initial investment in the portfolio associated with a selffinancing trading strategy generating $(S_T^1-K)^+$.

The incompleteness of a viable securities market model, however, implies the existence of different consistent price systems on the space of contingent claims (cf. Theorem 3.2.4). Accordingly, there are different valuations for a contingent claim that is not P^*-attainable. Those valuations are called *consistent with the prices of the given securities*. This chapter deals with the question whether it is possible to single out a specific consistent valuation and introduces a criterion for this purpose. This is achieved by discussing the possibility of generating a contingent claim, which is not P^*-attainable, by trading strategies that are not self-financing. A trading strategy ϕ is said *to generate the contingent claim* X if and only if (3.1.12) holds true.

In particular, we consider the model described in Section 3.3.2 and the contingent claim $(S_T^1 - K)^+$ associated with a European call option on a stock with price process (3.3.3). The possibility of generating the contingent claim $(S_T^1 - K)^+$ by trading strategies that are not self-financing is discussed. Several generating trading strategies are found and their associated gains or losses are calculated. It is examined whether there is a "best" trading strategy among all trading strategies that generate $(S_T^1 - K)^+$. A trading strategy is determined that has smallest expected squared gains or losses among all trading strategies that generate the contingent claim $(S_T^1 - K)^+$. The expected gains or losses associated with this trading strategy are zero. The initial investment in the portfolio associated with this optimal trading strategy gives a special consistent price.

The continuous-time securities market model of Section 3.3.2 is given. Lemma 4.3.1 shows that the contingent claim $X = (S_T^1 - K)^+$ is not P^*-attainable in this model. How should this contingent claim be valued? BLACK (1976b) comments on this problem as follows:

"If the volatility changes randomly in ways that don't depend on the stock price, then people may want to use options to bet on volatility changes, and the formulas will have to be changed in ways that we don't yet understand."

BLACK (1976b), p. 177

If a contingent claim is not P^*-attainable in the given model, it might be P^*-attainable in an extended model, which results from the given one after having introduced additional securities. This means that the given model is embedded in an extended securities market model with the aim of deriving preference-free valuations in the extended model. This approach to the valuation of contingent claims is already mentioned by COX/ROSS (1976a):

"Suppose that along with the stock and the option there are m-1 other assets that jump with the stock. The additional assets that are brought in for spanning the option could be other stocks or even other options - it does not really matter for pricing: it is only important to know that a hedge can be formed. If it can, then we can evaluate .[the call option] with any convenient equilibrium model, and usually risk neutrality proves to be most practical."

COX/ROSS (1976a), p. 396

For the model considered a further security price process can be defined by

$$S^2 := 1_{[0,t_0)}(\theta^*\sigma_1 + (1-\theta^*)\sigma_2) + 1_{[t_0,T]}(\sigma_1 1_A + \sigma_2 1_{A^c}) \tag{6.1}$$

S^2 represents the possibility to bet on the outcome of the event at time t_0. Obviously, (6.1) defines a square-integrable martingale. Furthermore,

$$H_0^{2,d}(P^*) = L(S^2 - S_0^2)$$

which yields

$$L(S^0, S^1, S^2) = H^2(P^*)$$

in combination with $H^{2,c}(P^*) = L(S^o,S^1)$. The extended securities market model made up of the same probability space (Ω,F,P) as the original model, the same set of trading dates [O,T], and securities with price processes (3.1.5), (3.3.3) and (6.1) is complete. Thus any contingent claim X can be priced uniquely in the extended model by its expected value $E^*[X]$ with respect to P^*.

The introduction of the new security reduces the number of martingale measures to the extreme case that $\mathbb{P}((S^o,S^1,S^2))$ is singleton. Note that $S_T^2/E^*[S_T^2]$ is the Radon-Nikodym derivative of a P^*-equivalent martingale measure for the security price process (S^o,S^1). Of course, for f_θ as in (4.3.4) $(E^*[f_\theta|F_t])$ could have taken the place of S^2. The choice of (6.1) has no influence on the valuation of the contingent claim X by means of its expected value $E^*[X]$ in the extended model. This also applies to the number of securities introduced in order to yield preference-free valuations of contingent claims in an extended model. Increasing the number of securities to be introduced will have no effect on the valuation of a contingent claim X by $E^*[X]$, if the extended model is already such that it yields preference-independent valuations according to the hedge approach. It does not make any difference whether there are L further securities with price processes $S^{K+1},\ldots,S^L$ such that $S^i \in L_{P^*}(S^o,\ldots,S^K)$, i=K+1,...,L holds true. A P^*-attainable contingent claim X in the extended model is always valued by $E^*[X]$. It follows that at least for valuation purposes the search for a minimal hedging portfolio, which is dealt with in the literature (cf. GESKE (1981), WHALEY (1981)), is superfluous.

A crucial feature of this extended hedge approach to the valuation of contingent claims is the dependence on the fixed equivalent martingale measure P^*. Starting from another equivalent martingale measure $\tilde{P}$ the procedure outlined above will yield the preference-free valuation $E^{\tilde{P}}[X]$ of X in a different extended model. Of course, the security to be introduced might differ from the one with the price process (6.1). Valuing contingent claims in the given model by the preference-free valuations that they might have in an extended model represents a specific preference-dependent approach to the valuation of contingent claims. The dependence on preferences is expressed by the equivalent martingale measure chosen. Theorem 3.2.4 and in particular its proof (cf. HARRISON/KREPS (1979), pp. 386) show that different equivalent martingale measures represent preferences of different agents. Thus depending on the equivalent martingale measure chosen different preference-dependent valuations of a contingent claim will result from the extended hedge approach. Consequently, we do not agree with COX/ ROSS (1976a), who argue:

> "Even though additional assets were required, then . [the value of the call option] still is simply the discounted expected value of max $\{S_T - K, 0\}$, and as such depends only on S..."
>
> COX/ROSS (1976a), p. 396

Any P^*-attainable contingent claim X in an extended model can be generated in a selffinancing way by a trading strategy in the securities of the extended model, yielding the valuation $E^*[X]$. This preference-dependent valuation resulting from the extended hedge approach has another interpretation, which might be of interest for the purpose of hedging. We consider the set $\hat{\Psi}_{P^*}$ of trading strategies defined by

$$\hat{\Psi}_{P^*} := \{ \phi \mid \phi \text{ predictable, } E^*[\int_0^T (\phi^k)^2 d[S^k,S^k]] < \infty,\ k\in\{1,...,K\} \}$$

and a trading strategy $\phi \in \hat{\Psi}_{P^*}$ generating the contingent claim X in the given model. If ϕ fulfills (3.1.12) but not $V(\phi) = \int \phi\, dS$, there are gains or losses associated with it. We will generally refer to those gains or losses as costs and denote them by $C(\phi)$, i.e.

$$C_t(\phi) = V_t(\phi) - \int_0^t \phi dS \qquad \forall t \in [0,T].$$

Of course, a selffinancing trading strategy will give rise to zero costs. Provided that the costs up to time T associated with a trading strategy $\phi \in \hat{\Psi}_{P^*}$ fulfilling (3.1.12) are zero on average, the initial investment in the corresponding portfolio equals $E^*[X]$, i.e. $E^*[C_T(\phi)] = 0$ implies

$$\begin{aligned} E^*[X] &= E^*[V_T(\phi)] \\ &= E^*[\int_0^T \phi dS] + E^*[C_T(\phi)] \\ &= V_0(\phi) . \end{aligned}$$

Thus $E^*[X]$ might be interpreted as the initial investment associated with a generating trading strategy that has average costs of zero. Do such trading strategies exist? Theorem 6.2 below gives an affirmative answer to this question.

Before addressing the question of existence we indicate how one might actually obtain generating trading strategies. For the securities market model given in Section 3.3.2 we determine generating trading strategies of the contingent claim $(S_T^1 - K)^+$. Since the extended securities market model based on (S^o, S^1, S^2) is complete, there exist predictable ψ^i, i=1,2,3, that fulfill the usual integrability conditions such that

$$(S_T^1 - K)^+ = \psi_T^o + \psi_T^1 S_T^1 + \psi_T^2 S_T^2$$

and

$$\psi^o + \psi^1 S^1 + \psi^2 S^2 = \psi_o^o + \int \psi^1 dS^1 + \int \psi^2 dS^2 \qquad (6.2)$$

holds true. As in Lemma 4.2.3 we consider the square integrable P^*-martingale (X_t) associated with $X := (S_T^1 - K)^+$, i.e.

$$X_t := E^*[(S_T^1 - K)^+ | F_t] \quad .$$

A natural candidate for a generating trading strategy would be the trading strategy that has the same components as ψ whenever possible and a zero component that accounts for the generating property, i.e.

$$\phi_t^o := (X_o - \psi_o^1 S_o^1)\, 1_{\{O\}}(t) + (X_{t-} - \psi_t^1 S_{t-}^1)\, 1_{(O,T]}(t) \quad \forall\ t \in [O,T] \qquad (6.3)$$

$$\phi_t^1 := \psi_t^1 \qquad \forall t \in [O,T] \qquad (6.4)$$

Note that $\phi := (\phi^o, \phi^1)$ is an element of $\hat{\Psi}_{P^*}$. ϕ generates the contingent claim, since (6.2), the property

$$\Delta(\int \psi^k dS^k)_t = \psi_t^k \, \Delta S_t^k$$

of stochastic integrals and the continuity of S^1 and S^2 for $t > t_o$ imply

$$X - X_{T-} = \Delta V_T(\psi) = \psi^1 \Delta S_T^1 + \psi^2 \Delta S_T^2 = O.$$

In order to determine ϕ we may proceed as in Example 4.1.8. The price process S^1 can be written in the form

$$S_t^1 = \begin{cases} Y_t^1 & t \leqq t_o \\ 1_A Y_t^1 + 1_{A^c} Y_t^2 & t > t_o \end{cases}$$

where Y^i, i=1,2 is defined by

$$dY^i = \tau_i Y^i \, dW$$

with

$$\tau_i(t) := \sigma_o 1_{[0,t_o]}(t) + \sigma_i 1_{(t_o,T]}(t), \quad i=1,2$$

and initial conditions S_o^1. Using the notation

$$\tau_i^*(t) := \int_t^T \tau_i^2(s)ds$$

the conditional expectation can be determined as follows

$$E^*[(S_T^1 - K)^+ | F_t] = E^*[1_A (Y_T^1 - K)^+ | F_t] + E^*[1_{A^c} (Y_T^2 - K)^+ | F_t]$$

$$= E^*[1_A \, Y_T^1 \, 1_{\{Y_T^1 > K\}} | F_t] + E^*[1_{A^c} \, Y_T^2 \, 1_{\{Y_T^2 > K\}} | F_t]$$

$$- K \, E^*[1_A \, 1_{\{Y_T^1 > K\}} | F_t] - K \, E^*[1_{A^c} \, 1_{\{Y_T^2 > K\}} | F_t]$$

$$= 1_{[0,t_o)} (S_t^1 (\theta^* \Phi(\frac{\ln\frac{S_t^1}{K} + \frac{\tau_1^*(t)}{2}}{\sqrt{\tau_1^*(t)}}) + (1-\theta^*)\Phi(\frac{\ln\frac{S_t^1}{K} + \frac{\tau_2^*(t)}{2}}{\sqrt{\tau_2^*(t)}}))$$

$$- K \, (\theta^* \Phi(\frac{\ln\frac{S_t^1}{K} - \frac{\tau_1^*(t)}{2}}{\sqrt{\tau_1^*(t)}}) + (1-\theta^*)\Phi(\frac{\ln\frac{S_t^1}{K} - \frac{\tau_2^*(t)}{2}}{\sqrt{\tau_2^*(t)}})))$$

$$+ 1_{[t_o,T]} (S_t^1 (1_A \Phi(\frac{\ln\frac{S_t^1}{K} + \frac{\tau_1^*(t)}{2}}{\sqrt{\tau_1^*(t)}}) + 1_{A^c} \, \Phi(\frac{\ln\frac{S_t^1}{K} + \frac{\tau_2^*(t)}{2}}{\sqrt{\tau_2^*(t)}}))$$

$$- K \, (1_A \, \Phi(\frac{\ln\frac{S_t^1}{K} - \frac{\tau_1^*(t)}{2}}{\sqrt{\tau_1^*(t)}}) + 1_{A^c} \, \Phi(\frac{\ln\frac{S_t^1}{K} - \frac{\tau_2^*(t)}{2}}{\sqrt{\tau_2^*(t)}})))$$

The conditional expectation $E^*[(S_T^1 - K)^+|F_t]$ just obtained suggests the following first component of a generating trading strategy.

$$\phi_t^1 := \begin{cases} \theta^*\Phi\left(\dfrac{\ln\frac{S_t^1}{K} + \frac{\tau_1^*(t)}{2}}{\sqrt{\tau_1^*(t)}}\right) + (1-\theta^*)\Phi\left(\dfrac{\ln\frac{S_t^1}{K} + \frac{\tau_2^*(t)}{2}}{\sqrt{\tau_2^*(t)}}\right) & t \leq t_o \\ 1_A\Phi\left(\dfrac{\ln\frac{S_t^1}{K} + \frac{\tau_1^*(t)}{2}}{\sqrt{\tau_1^*(t)}}\right) + 1_{A^c}\,\Phi\left(\dfrac{\ln\frac{S_t^1}{K} + \frac{\tau_2^*(t)}{2}}{\sqrt{\tau_2^*(t)}}\right) & t > t_o \end{cases} \tag{6.5}$$

According to (6.3) the associated component ϕ^o is given by

$$\phi_t^o := \begin{cases} -K\left(\theta^*\Phi\left(\dfrac{\ln\frac{S_t^1}{K} - \frac{\tau_1^*(t)}{2}}{\sqrt{\tau_1^*(t)}}\right) + (1-\theta^*)\Phi\left(\dfrac{\ln\frac{S_t^1}{K} - \frac{\tau_2^*(t)}{2}}{\sqrt{\tau_2^*(t)}}\right)\right) & t \leq t_o \\ -K\left(1_A\Phi\left(\dfrac{\ln\frac{S_t^1}{K} - \frac{\tau_1^*(t)}{2}}{\sqrt{\tau_1^*(t)}}\right) + 1_{A^c}\,\Phi\left(\dfrac{\ln\frac{S_t^1}{K} - \frac{\tau_2^*(t)}{2}}{\sqrt{\tau_2^*(t)}}\right)\right) & t > t_o \end{cases} \tag{6.6}$$

ϕ defined by (6.5) and (6.6) is an admissible generating trading strategy, i.e. $\phi \in \hat{\Psi}_P{}^*$.

Now we consider the costs that are associated with ϕ. For that reason, we first determine the stochastic integral $\phi_o^o + \int\phi^1 dS^1$. Note that ϕ can be written in the form

$$\phi_t := \begin{cases} \theta^*\beta_t(\tau_1) + (1-\theta^*)\beta_t(\tau_2) & t \leq t_o \\ 1_A\,\beta_t(\tau_1) + 1_{A^c}\,\beta_t(\tau_2) & t > t_o \end{cases} \tag{6.7}$$

In (6.7) $\beta(\tau_i)$, i=1,2, denotes the selffinancing trading strategy that generates the contingent claim $(Y_T^i - K)^+$ associated with a European call option written on a stock with price process Y^i, exercise price K and expiration date T, i.e.

$$\beta_t^o(\tau_i) := -K\,\Phi\left(\frac{\ln\frac{Y_t^i}{K} - \frac{1}{2}\tau_i^*(t)}{\sqrt{\tau_i^*(t)}}\right)$$

$$\beta_t^1(\tau_i) := \Phi\left(\frac{\ln\frac{Y_t^i}{K} + \frac{1}{2}\tau_i^*(t)}{\sqrt{\tau_i^*(t)}}\right)$$

Since all integrands considered are bounded, the standard properties of the stochastic integral (cf. the Appendix) yield

$$\int_o^t \phi dS = \int_o^t \{1_{[0,t_o]}(s)(\theta^*\beta_s(\tau_1) + (1-\theta^*)\beta_s(\tau_2))$$

$$+ 1_{(t_o,T]}(1_A\beta_s(\tau_1) + 1_{A^c}\beta_s(\tau_2))\}\, dS$$

$$= \int_o^t (\theta^* 1_{[0,t_o]} + 1_A 1_{(t_o,T]})\beta_s(\tau_1)dS$$

$$+ \int_o^t ((1-\theta^*)1_{[0,t_o]} + 1_{A^c} 1_{(t_o,T]})\beta_s(\tau_2)dS$$

$$= 1_{[0,t_o]}(t)\{\theta^* \int_o^t \beta_s(\tau_1)dS + (1-\theta^*) \int_o^t \beta_s(\tau_2)dS\}$$

$$+ 1_{(t_o,T]}(t)\{(\theta^*-1_A)(\int_o^{t_o} \beta_s(\tau_1)dS - \int_o^{t_o} \beta_s(\tau_2)dS)$$

$$+ 1_A \int_o^t \beta_s(\tau_1)dS + 1_{A^c} \int_o^t \beta_s(\tau_2)dS\}$$

$$= 1_{[0,t_o]}(t)\{\theta^* \int_o^t \beta_s(\tau_1)dY^1 + (1-\theta^*) \int_o^t \beta_s(\tau_2)dY^1\}$$

$$+ 1_{(t_o,T]}(t)\{(\theta^*-1_A)(\int_o^{t_o} \beta_s(\tau_1)dY^1 - \int_o^{t_o} \beta_s(\tau_2)dY^1)$$

$$+ 1_A \int_o^t \beta_s(\tau_1)dY^1 + 1_{A^c} \int_o^t \beta_s(\tau_2)dY^2\}$$

Using the fact that $\beta(\tau_i)$, i=1,2, is selffinancing, i.e.

$$V(\beta(\tau_i)) = \int \beta(\tau_i)dY^i$$

we get for $t \leq t_0$

$$\int_0^t \phi dS = \theta^*(V_t(\beta(\tau_1)) + (1-\theta^*)(V_t(\beta(\tau_2))$$

$$= V_t(\theta^*\beta(\tau_1) + (1-\theta^*)\beta(\tau_2))$$

$$= V_t(\phi)$$

For $t > t_0$ the stochastic integral reduces to

$$\int_0^t \phi dS = (\theta^* - 1_A)(V_{t_0}(\beta(\tau_1)) - V_{t_0}(\beta(\tau_2))$$

$$+ 1_A V_t(\beta(\tau_1)) + 1_{A^c} V_t(\beta(\tau_2))$$

$$= (\theta^* - 1_A)(V_{t_0}(\beta(\tau_1)) - V_{t_0}(\beta(\tau_2))) + V_t(\phi)$$

Thus the costs associated with the generating trading strategy ϕ are given by

$$C_t(\phi) = 1_{(t_0,T]}(t)\{(1_A - \theta^*)(V_{t_0}(\beta(\tau_1)) - V_{t_0}(\beta(\tau_2)))\}$$

The costs associated with ϕ do only occur at time t_0 and depend on the outcome of the random effect. At all other times the trading strategy ϕ does not require nor generate funds.

Are there other admissible trading strategies that generate the contingent claim $(S_T^1 - K)^+$? Any trading strategy that equals ϕ on

$(t_1,T]$ for a t_1 with $t_o < t_1 < T$ will do. In particular, this applies to the naively employed original BLACK/SCHOLES trading strategy for a process that follows a geometric Brownian motion with variance parameter σ_o up to time t_o without taking into account that there will be a change in variance. This trading strategy is given by

$$\phi_t^{BS} := \begin{cases} \beta_t(\sigma_o) & t \leq t_o \\ 1_A \beta_t(\tau_1) + 1_{A^c}\, \beta_t(\tau_2) & t > t_o \end{cases}$$

The costs associated with ϕ^{BS} can be determined. A calculation similar to the one given above yields

$$C_t(\phi^{BS}) = 1_{(t_o,T]}(t)\{1_A(V_{t_o}(\beta(\tau_1)) - V_{t_o}(\beta(\sigma_o))) + 1_{A^c}(V_{t_o}(\beta(\tau_2)) - V_{t_o}(\beta(\sigma_o)))\}$$

What is a reasonable criterion to discriminate between those competing generating trading strategies ? The following lemma addresses this problem and reports properties of the trading strategy ϕ.

<u>6.1 Lemma</u>

The expected costs up to time T of the generating trading strategy ϕ are zero, i.e.

$$E^*[C_T(\phi)] = 0.$$

ϕ is the trading strategy that has smallest expected squared costs up to time T among all trading strategies $\tilde{\phi} \in \hat{\Psi}_{P^*}$ that generate $(S_T^1 - K)^+$, i.e.

$$E^*[(C_T(\phi))^2] = \min_{\substack{\tilde{\phi}\in\hat{\Psi}_{P^*} \\ V_T(\tilde{\phi})=X}} E^*[(C_T(\tilde{\phi}))^2] \tag{6.8}$$

<u>Proof:</u>

$E^*[C_T(\phi)] = 0$ follows immediately from the special form of $C_T(\phi)$ using the stochastic independence of 1_A and Y^i, $i=1,2$. Now consider any trading strategy $\tilde{\phi} \in \hat{\Psi}_{P^*}$ that generates $(S_T^1 - K)^+$. We get

$$(S_T^1 - K)^+ = V_T(\tilde{\phi}) = V_T(\phi) = \int_0^T \phi dS + C_T(\phi)$$

and

$$C_T(\tilde{\phi}) = V_T(\tilde{\phi}) - \int_0^T \tilde{\phi}dS \ .$$

This implies

$$E^*[(C_T(\tilde{\phi}))^2] = E^*[(V_T(\tilde{\phi}) - \int_0^T \tilde{\phi}dS)^2]$$

$$= E^*[(\int_0^T(\phi - \tilde{\phi})dS + C_T(\phi))^2]$$

$$= E^*[(\int_0^T(\phi - \tilde{\phi})dS)^2] + 2E^*[(C_T(\phi))(\int_0^T(\phi - \tilde{\phi})dS)]$$

$$+ E^*[(C_T(\phi))^2] \quad .$$

We only have to show that

$$E^*[(C_T(\phi))(\int_0^T(\phi - \tilde{\phi})dS)] = 0 \ .$$

Using the standard properties of conditional expectation and the stochastic independence of 1_A and $\int_0^{t_0}(\phi - \tilde{\phi})dS$ we obtain

$$E^*[(C_T(\phi))(\int_0^T(\phi - \tilde{\phi})dS)]$$

$$= E^*[E^*[(C_T(\phi))(\int_0^T(\phi - \tilde{\phi})dS)|F_{t_0}]]$$

$$= E^*[(C_T(\phi))(E^*[\int_0^T(\phi - \tilde{\phi})dS|F_{t_0}])]$$

$$= E^*[(C_T(\phi))(\int_0^{t_0}(\phi - \tilde{\phi})dS)]$$

$$= (E^*[1_A-\theta^*])(E^*[(V_{t_0}(\beta(\tau_1))-V_{t_0}(\beta(\tau_2)))(\int_0^{t_0}(\phi-\tilde{\phi})dS)])$$

$$= 0 \quad \square$$

Naturally the question arises to what extent the results of Lemma 6.1 are due to the specific structure of the securities market model considered. The following theorem shows that under suitable regularity conditions the existence of a generating trading strategy that minimizes expected squared costs can be guaranteed.

6.2 Theorem

Consider a security price process S and a contingent claim X such that $S_{T-} = S_T$ a.s. and $X_{T-} = X$ a.s. holds true. There exists a trading strategy $\phi := (\phi^O,\dots,\phi^K) \in \hat{\Psi}_{P*}$ generating X that has smallest expected squared costs up to time T among all trading strategies $\tilde{\phi} \in \hat{\Psi}_{P*}$ generating X. The expected costs up to time T associated with ϕ are zero.

Proof

We consider the square integrable martingale $U := (U_t)_{t\in[O,T]}$, which is defined by $U_t := E^*[X|\mathcal{F}_t]$. By Lemma 4.2.1, $\mathcal{L}_{P*}(S^O,\dots,S^K)$ is a stable subspace of $\mathcal{H}^2(P^*)$. Then U has a unique decomposition

$$U = M + N ,$$

where $M \in \mathcal{L}_{P*}(S^O,\dots,S^K)$ and $N \in (\mathcal{L}_{P*}(S^O,\dots,S^K))^{\perp}$ holds true. Necessarily, we have $N_O = E^*[N_T] = O$. Because of the special structure of $\mathcal{L}_{P*}(S^O,\dots,S^K)$ there exist $\phi_O^O \in \mathbb{R}$ and predictable processes ϕ^k, $k \in \{1,\dots,K\}$ fulfilling $E^*[\int_O^T (\phi^k)^2 d[S^k,S^k]] < \infty$ such that M is of the form

$$M = \phi_O^O + \sum_{k=1}^{K} \int \phi^k \, dS^k . \tag{6.9}$$

Define ϕ^O by

$$\phi_t^O = \phi_O^O \, 1_{\{O\}}(t) + 1_{(O,T]}(t)(U_{t-} - \sum_{k=1}^{K} \phi_t^k S_{t-}^k) \tag{6.10}$$

ϕ is an admissible trading strategy, i.e. $\phi \in \hat{\Psi}_{P*}$, that generates the contingent claim X.
Now consider any trading strategy $\tilde{\phi} \in \hat{\Psi}_{P*}$ generating X. We get

$$X = V_T(\tilde{\phi}) = V_T(\phi) = \int_O^T \phi dS + N_T \tag{6.11}$$

and

$$C_T(\tilde{\phi}) = V_T(\tilde{\phi}) - \int_0^T \tilde{\phi}\,dS \ . \tag{6.12}$$

Using the strong orthogonality of N to $L_{P*}(S^0,\ldots,S^K)$, (6.11) and (6.12) imply

$$E^*[(C_T(\tilde{\phi}))^2] = E^*[(\int_0^T \phi\,dS - \int_0^T \tilde{\phi}\,dS + N_T)^2]$$

$$= E^*[(\int_0^T (\phi - \tilde{\phi})dS)^2] + E^*[N_T^2]$$

$$\geqq E^*[N_T^2] = E^*[(C_T(\phi))^2]$$

Since $C_T(\phi) = V_T(\phi) - \int_0^T \phi\,dS = N_T$, we get

$$E^*[C_T(\phi)] = E^*[N_T] = N_0 = 0 \ \square$$

7 Conclusion

This monograph developed the concept of arbitrage pricing of contingent claims within the framework of a continuous-time securities market model. A finite number of securities are considered which are being traded between an initial date zero and a final date T. The continuous-time securities market model consists of a probability space $(\Omega,\mathcal{F},P)$, where elements ω of Ω represent states of the world, the set $[0,T]$ of trading dates of the given securities, an information structure and a security price process that represents the prices of the given securities. The model considered differs from the one of HARRISON/KREPS(1979) in that it allows for arbitrary trading dates between zero and T and continuous-time trading.

The arbitrage pricing concept is based on generating the contingent claim by means of a continuously adjusted portfolio in the given securities. One tries to determine a portfolio that produces exactly the same pattern of cash-flows as the contingent claim and that apart from the initial investment neither requires funds to be invested nor allows for withdrawals. Such a portfolio is called self-financing and generating the contingent claim. The valuation principle rests on the following argument. If arbitrage opportunities are excluded, then there is a unique price for every contingent claim that can be generated by a self-financing portfolio. This price is given by the initial investment in the generating portfolio. In contrast to the continuous-time securities market models to be found in the literature the approach chosen in this monograph is based on approximations. The basic continuous-time definitions and concepts are introduced by limit arguments using an economically meaningful convergence concept. The approximating models are characterized by a finite number of trading dates in the given securities. This approach has several advantages. First, it avoids the definitorial problems associated with the continuous-time case (cf. HARRISON/PLISKA (1981), p. 257). Secondly, arguing by means of approximations might clarify the valuation principle based on arbitrage considerations. The discrete-time setting, however, does not suffice for valuation purposes as is shown in Example 4.6.1. Finally, the approach chosen yields explicit approximations of continuous-time self-financing trading strategies by means of simple self-financing trading strategies as well as approximations of attainable contingent claims by means of simply attainable contingent claims. Approximations of this kind are of interest in empirical studies. They may be used for actual valuation purposes as well as for the purpose of hedging.

In contrast ot most work in the literature, the present monograph explicitly accounts for incomplete securities market models, i.e. it allows for contingent claims that cannot be generated by self-financing portfolios in the given securities. For arbitrary viable securities market models a characterization of attainable contingent claims is obtained and the prices of attainable contingent claims are determined. It turns out that those prices are given as expected values of the corresponding contingent claims with respect to an equivalent martingale measure.

A crucial feature of contingent claim pricing by means of generating self-financing portfolios is the dependence on the given securities market model. Whether or not there exists a self-financing generating portfolio for a specific contingent claim essentially depends on the distribution of the given securities. This is illustrated by means of the contingent claim associated with a European call option written on a stock with price process (5.0.6) and (5.0.7). If the variance parameter is replaced by a random variable,this contingent claim cannot be generated any more by a self-financing portfolio in the given securities. As to this problem there are at least two directions for future research. The first concerns complete securities market models whereas the second deals with the question of how to value contingent claims that cannot be generated by self-financing portfolios in the given securities.

Further research on complete securities market models should provide an answer to the question which security price processes yield complete securities markets. Knowing this class of security price processes would reduce the valuation problem to the question, whether the price process of the given securities could adequately be described by elements of this class. Ultimately, however, this question could only be answered by empirical studies.

The pricing of contingent claims that cannot be generated by self-financing portfolios in the given securities merits further study. A first attempt to solve this problem is reported in this monograph. Chapter 6 considers the possibility of generating a contingent claim by portfolios that are not necessarily self-financing. It is examined whether there is a "best" portfolio among all admissible portfolios generating the contingent claim. Under suitable regularity conditions it is shown that for every contingent claim there exists a generating portfolio that has expected costs of zero and has smallest expected squared costs up to time T among all admissible generating portfolios. The initial investment in this optimal portfolio gives a special consistent price for the contingent claim. This consistent price could also be interpreted as a valuation resulting from the arbitrage pricing approach applied to an extended securities market model. A different attempt to deal with contingent claims in incomplete securities markets is given in FÖLLMER/SONDERMANN (1985). FÖLLMER/SONDERMANN do not consider the pricing of contingent claims. They are only interested in hedging of non-redundant contingent claims. For that purpose they introduce trading strategies with associated cost processes being martingales.

References

ANANTHANARAYANAN, A.L. and E. SCHWARTZ (1980), "Retractable and extendible bonds: The Canadian Experience", Journal of Finance, 35,31-47

ARROW, K.J. (1964), "The role of securities in the optimal allocation of risk-bearing", Review of Economic Studies, 31, 91-96

ARROW, K.J. and M.D. INTRILIGATOR (1982), (eds.), Handbook of mathematical economics, Vol. 2, North Holland, Amsterdam, New York, Oxford 1982

BACHELIER, L. (1900), "Theory of speculation", in: The random character of stock market prices, edited by P.H. Cootner, MIT Press, Cambridge, Ma 1964, 17-78

BALL, C.A. and W.N. TOROUS (1983a), "A simplified jump process for common stock returns", Journal of Financial and Quantitative Analysis, 18, 53-65

BALL, C.A. and W.N. TOROUS (1983b), "Parameter estimation of the compound events model for security prices", Discussion Paper, Graduate School of Business, University of Michigan, 1983

BAUER, H. (1974), Wahrscheinlichkeitstheorie und Grundzüge der Maßtheorie, Walter de Gruyter Verlag, Berlin 1974

BECKERS, S. (1980), "The constant elasticity of variance model and its implications for option pricing", Journal of Finance, 35, 661-673

BECKERS, S. (1981), "Standard deviations implied in option prices as predictors of future stock price variability", Journal of Banking and Finance, 5, 363-381

BERGMAN, Y. (1981), "A characterization of self-financing portfolio strategies", Discussion Paper, School of Business Administration, UC Berkeley 1981

BHATTACHARYA, M. (1980), "Empirical properties of the Black-Scholes formula under ideal conditions", Journal of Financial and Quantitative Analysis, 15, 1081-1105

BHATTACHARYA, S. (1981), "Notes on multiperiod valuation and the pricing of options", Journal of Finance, 36, 163-180

BICK, A. (1982), "Comments on the valuation of derivative assets", Journal of Financial Economics, 10, 331-345

BLACK, F. (1976 a),"The pricing of commodity contracts", Journal of Financial Economics, 3, 167-179

BLACK, F. (1976b), Studies of stock price volatility changes, American Statistical Association, Proceedings of the Business and Economic Statistics Section 1976, 177-186

BLACK, F. and J. COX (1976), " Valuing corporate securities: some effects of bond indenture provisions", Journal of Finance, 31, 351-367

BLACK, F. and M. SCHOLES (1972), "The valuation of option contracts and a test of market efficiency", Journal of Finance, 27, 399-417

BLACK, F. and M. SCHOLES (1973), "The pricing of options and corporate liabilities", Journal of Political Economy, 81, 637-654

BLATTBERG, R. and N. GONEDES (1974), "A comparison of the stable and Student distributions as statistical models for stock prices", Journal of Business, 47, 244-280

BLOMEYER, E. and R. KLEMKOSKY (1983), "Tests of market efficiency for American call options", in: Option pricing, edited by M. Brenner, Lexington 1983, 101-121

BONESS, A.J. (1964), "Elements of a theory of stock-option value", Journal of Political Economy, 72, 163-175

BONESS, J., CHEN, A. and S. JATUSIPITAK (1974), "Investigations of non-stationarity in prices", Journal of Business, 47, 518-537

BOOKSTABER, R.M. (1981), "Observed option mispricing and the nonsimultaneity of stock and option quotations", Journal of Business, 54, 141-155

BOYLE, P. and A. ANANTHANARAYANAN (1977), "The impact of variance estimation in option valuation models", Journal of Financial Economics, 5, 375-387

BOYLE, P. and D. EMANUEL (1980), "Discretely adjusted option hedges", Journal of Financial Economics, 8, 259-282

BRENNAN, M.J. (1979), "The pricing of contingent claims in discrete time models", Journal of Finance, 34, 53-68

BRENNAN, M.J. and E. SCHWARTZ (1977a), " The valuation of American put options", Journal of Finance, 32, 449-462

BRENNAN, M.J. and E. SCHWARTZ (1977b), "Convertible bonds: valuation and optimal strategies for call and conversion", Journal of Finance, 32, 1699-1715

BRENNAN, M.J. and E. SCHWARTZ (1978), "Finite difference methods and jump processes arising in the pricing of contingent claims: a synthesis", Journal of Financial and Quantitative Analysis, 13, 461-474

BRENNAN, M.J. and E. SCHWARTZ (1979), "A continuous time approach to the pricing of bonds", Journal of Banking and Finance, 3, 133-155

BRENNER, M. (1983), (ed.), Option pricing. Theory and applications, Lexington Books, Lexington, Ma 1983

CHAMBERLAIN, G. (1983), "Funds, factors, and diversification in arbitrage pricing models", Econometrica, 51, 1305-1323

CHAMBERLAIN, G. and M. ROTHSCHILD (1983), "Arbitrage, factor structure, and mean-variance analysis on large asset markets", Econometrica, 51, 1281-1304

CHIRAS, D. and S. MANASTER (1978), "The information content of option prices and a test of market efficiency", Journal of Financial Economics, 6, 213-234

CHOW, Y. and H. TEICHER (1978), Probability theory, independence, interchangeability, martingales, Springer Verlag, Berlin, Heidelberg, New York 1978

CHRISTIE,A. (1982), "The stochastic behaviour of common stock variances", Journal of Financial Economics, 10, 407-432

COOTNER, P. (1964), The random character of stock market prices, MIT Press, Cambridge, Ma. 1964

COX, J. and S. ROSS (1976a), "A survey of some new results in financial option pricing theory", Journal of Finance, 31, 383-402

COX, J. and S. ROSS (1976b), "The valuation of options for alternative stochastic processes", Journal of Financial Economics, 3, 145-166

COX, J., ROSS, S. and M. RUBINSTEIN (1979), "Option pricing: A simplified approach", Journal of Financial Economics, 7, 229-261

COX, J. and M. RUBINSTEIN (1983), "A survey of alternative option pricing models", in: Option pricing, edited by M. Brenner, Lexington, Ma. 1983, 3-33

DELLACHERIE, C. and P.-A. MEYER (1978), Probabilities and potential, North Holland, Amsterdam 1978

DELLACHERIE, C. and P.-A. MEYER (1982), Probabilities and potential B, North Holland, Amsterdam 1982

DUNFORD, N. and J.T. SCHWARTZ (1957), Linear operators, Part I: General theory, Interscience Publishers, New York 1957

ELLIOTT, R.J. (1982), Stochastic calculus and applications, Springer Verlag, Berlin, Heidelberg, New York 1982

FAMA, E. (1963), "Mandelbrot and the stable Paretian hypothesis", Journal of Business, 36, 420-429

FAMA, E. (1970), "Efficient capital markets: A review of theory and empirical work", Journal of Finance, 25, 383-417

FEIGER, G. and B. JACQUILLAT, (1979), "Currency option bonds, puts and calls on spot exchange and the hedging of contingent foreign earnings", Journal of Finance, 34, 1129-1139

FIELITZ, B. (1971), "Stationarity of random data: some implications for the distribution of stock price changes", Journal of Financial and Quantitative Analysis, 6, 1025-1034

FISCHER, S. (1978), "Call option pricing when the exercise price is uncertain, and the valuation of index bonds", Journal of Finance, 33, 169-176

FÖLLMER, H. and D. SONDERMANN (1985), "Hedging of non-redundant contingent claims", SFB 303 Discussion Paper No. B-3, University of Bonn, May 1985

GALAI, D. (1983), "A survey of empirical tests of option pricing models", in: Option pricing, edited by M. Brenner, Lexington Books, Lexington, Ma. 1983, 45-80

GALAI, D. and R. MASULIS (1976), "The option pricing model and the risk factor of stock", Journal of Financial Economics, 3, 53-81

GESKE, R. (1978), "The pricing of options with stochastic dividend yield", Journal of Finance, 33, 617-625

GESKE, R. (1979a), "A note on an analytical valuation formula for unprotected American call options on stocks with known dividends", Journal of Financial Economics, 7, 375-380

GESKE, R. (1979b), "The valuation of compound options", Journal of Financial Economics, 7, 63-81

GESKE, R. (1981), "Comments on Whaley's note", Journal of Financial Economics, 9, 213-215

GIHMAN, I.I. and A.V. SKOROHOD (1972), Stochastic differential equations, Springer Verlag, Berlin, Heidelberg, New York 1972

GLEIT, A. (1978), "Valuation of general contingent claims", Journal of Financial Economics, 6, 71-87

GOLDMAN, M.B., SOSIN, H. and M. GATTO (1979), "Path dependent options: buy at the low, sell at the high", Journal of Finance, 34, 1111-1127

GOULD, J. and D. GALAI (1974), "Transaction costs and the relationship between put and call prices", Journal of Financial Economics, 1, 105-129

GREENE, M. and B. FIELITZ (1977), "Long-term dependence in common stock returns", Journal of Financial Economics, 4, 339-349

HAKANSSON, N. (1978), "Welfare aspects of options and supershares", Journal of Finance, 33, 759-776

HAKANSSON, N. (1979), "The fantastic world of finance: progress and the free lunch", Journal of Financial and Quantitative Analysis, 14, 717-734

HALMOS, P. (1950), Measure theory, Van Nostrand, Princeton 1950

HARRISON, J. and D. KREPS (1979), "Martingales and arbitrage in multiperiod securities markets", Journal of Economic Theory, 20, 381-408

HARRISON, J. and S. PLISKA (1981), "Martingales and stochastic integrals in the theory of continuous trading", Stochastic Processes and their Applications, 11, 215-260

HARRISON, J. and S. PLISKA (1983), "A stochastic calculus model of continuous trading: complete markets", Stochastic Processes and their Applications,15, 313-316

HILDENBRAND, W. (1974), Core and equilibria of a large economy, Princeton University Press, Princeton 1974

JACOD, J. (1979), Calcul stochastique et problèmes de martingales, Springer Verlag, Berlin, Heidelberg, New York 1979

JACOD, J. and M. Yor (1977), "Étude des solutions extrémales et représentation intégrale des solutions pour certains problèmes de martingales", Z. Wahrscheinlichkeitstheorie verw. Gebiete, 38, 83-125

JARROW, R. and A. RUDD (1982), "Approximate option valuation for arbitrary stochastic processes", Journal of Financial Economics, 10, 347-369

JARROW, R. and A. RUDD (1983), "Tests of an approximate option valuation formula", in: Option pricing, edited by M. Brenner, Lexington, Ma. 1983, 81-100

KREPS, D. (1980), "Multiperiod securities and the efficient allocation of risk: A comment on the Black-Scholes option pricing model", Technical Report No. 306, Institute for Mathematical Studies in the Social Sciences, Stanford University 1980

KREPS, D. (1981), "Arbitrage and equilibrium in economies with infinitely many commodities", Journal of Mathematical Economics, 8, 15-35

LATANE, H. and R. RENDLEMAN (1976), "Standard deviations of stock price ratios implied in option prices", Journal of Finance, 31, 369-381

LEE, W., RAO, R. and J. AUCHMUTY (1981), "Option pricing in a lognormal securities market with discrete trading", Journal of Financial Economics, 9, 75-101

LINTNER, J. (1965), "The valuation of risk assets and the selection of risk investment in stock portfolios and capital budgets", Review of Economics and Statistics, 47, 13-37

MACBETH, J. and L. MERVILLE (1979), "An empirical examination of the Black-Scholes call option pricing model", Journal of Finance, 34, 1173-1186

MACBETH, J. and L. MERVILLE (1980), "Tests of the Black-Scholes and Cox call option valuation models", Journal of Finance, 35, 285-303

MANASTER, S. and G. KOEHLER (1982), "The calculation of implied variances from the Black-Scholes model: A note", Journal of Finance, 37, 227-230

MANASTER, S. and R. RENDLEMAN (1982), "Option prices as predictors of equilibrium stock prices", Journal of Finance, 37, 1043-1057

MANDELBROT, B. (1963), "The variation of certain speculative prices", Journal of Business, 36, 394-419

MERTON, R. (1971), "Optimum consumption and portfolio rules in a continuous-time model", Journal of Economic Theory, 3, 373-413

MERTON, R. (1973), "Theory of rational option pricing", Bell Journal of Economics and Management Science, 4, 141-183

MERTON, R. (1976a), "The impact on option pricing of specification error in the underlying stock price returns", Journal of Finance, 31, 333-350

MERTON, R. (1976b), "Option pricing when underlying stock returns are discontinuous", Journal of Financial Economics, 3, 125-144

MERTON, R. (1977a), "On the pricing of contingent claims and the Modigliani-Miller theorem", Journal of Financial Economics, 5, 241-249

MERTON, R. (1977b), " An analytic derivation of the cost of deposit insurance and loan guarantees", Journal of Banking and Finance, 1, 3-11

MERTON, R. (1982), "On the microeconomic theory of investment under uncertainty", in: Handbook of mathematical economics, Vol. 2, edited by K.J. Arrow and M. Intriligator, North-Holland, Amsterdam, New York, Oxford 1982, 601-669

MERTON, R. and P. SAMUELSON (1974), "Fallacy of the log-normal approximation to optimal portfolio decision-making over many periods", Journal of Financial Economics, 1, 67-94

MERTON, R., SCHOLES, M. and M. GLADSTEIN (1978), "The returns and risk of alternative call option portfolio investment strategies", Journal of Business, 51, 183-242

METIVIER, M. (1982), Semimartingales, A course on stochastic processes, de Gruyter, Berlin, New York 1982

MOSSIN, J. (1966), "Equilibrium in a capital asset market", Econometrica, 34, 768-783

MÜLLER, S. (1983), "On a characterization of complete securities markets", SFB 21 Discussion Paper No. 141, University of Bonn, October 1983

MÜLLER, S. (1984), "On the valuation of contingent claims in arbitrage pricing models", SFB 21 Discussion Paper No. 142, University of Bonn, January 1984

OLDFIELD, G., ROGALSKI, R. and R. JARROW (1977), "An autoregressive jump process for common stock returns", Journal of Financial Economics, 5, 389-418

PARKINSON, M. (1977), "Option pricing: The American put", Journal of Business, 50, 21-36

RADNER, R. (1972), "Existence of equilibrium of plans, prices, and price expectations in a sequence of markets", Econometrica, 40, 289-303

RADNER, R. (1982), "Equilibrium under uncertainty", in: Handbook of mathematical economics, Vol. 2, edited by K.J. Arrow and M. Intriligator, North-Holland, Amsterdam, New York, Oxford 1982, 923-1006

RICHARD, S. (1978), "An arbitrage model of the term structure of interest rates", Journal of Financial Economics, 6, 33-57

ROLL, R. (1977), "An analytic valuation formula for unprotected American call options on stocks with known dividends", Journal of Financial Economics, 5, 251-258

ROOTZEN, H. (1980), "Limit distributions for the error in approximations of stochastic integrals", Annals of Probability, 8, 241-251

ROSS, S. (1976), "The arbitrage theory of capital asset pricing", Journal of Economic Theory, 13, 341-360

RUBINSTEIN, M. (1976), "The valuation of uncertain income streams and the pricing of options", Bell Journal of Economics, 7, 407-425

RUBINSTEIN, M. (1983), "Displaced diffusion option pricing", Journal of Finance, 38, 213-217

SAMUELSON, P. (1965a), "Rational theory of warrant pricing", Industrial Management Review, 6, 13-31, in: The collected scientific papers of Paul A. Samuelson, Vol. III, edited by R. Merton, MIT Press, Cambridge, Ma. 1972, 791-810

SAMUELSON, P. (1965b), "Proof that properly anticipated prices fluctuate randomly", Industrial Management Review, 6, 41-50, in: The collected scientific papers of Paul A. Samuelson, Vol. III, edited by R. Merton, MIT Press, Cambridge, Ma. 1972,782-790

SAMUELSON, P. (1970), "The fundamental approximation theorem of portfolio analysis in terms of means, variances and higher moments", Review of Economic Studies, 37, 537-542

SAMUELSON, P. (1973), "Mathematics of speculative price", SIAM Review, 15, 1-42

SHARPE, W. (1964), "Capital asset prices: a theory of market equilibrium under conditions of risk", Journal of Finance, 19, 425-442

SHARPE, W. (1978), Investment, Prentice-Hall, Eaglewood Cliffs 1978

SMITH, C. (1976), "Option pricing, A review", Journal of Financial Economics, 3, 3-51

SMITH, C. (1977), "Alternative methods of raising capital: rights versus underwritten offerings", Journal of Financial Economics, 5, 273-307

SMITH, C. (1979), "Applications of option pricing analysis", in: Handbook of Financial Economics, edited by J. Bicksler, North Holland, Amsterdam 1979, 79-121

SONDERMANN, D. (1974), "Temporary competitive equilibrium under uncertainty",in: Allocation under uncertainty: Equilibrium and optimality", edited by J. Drèze, Macmillan Press, London 1974, 229-253

SONDERMANN, D. (1985), "Kurssicherungsverfahren: Hedgen von Optionen", in: Ökonomische Prognose-, Entscheidungs- und Gleichgewichtsmodelle, Abschlußbericht des SFB 21, edited by W. Krelle, Weinheim, to appear

SPRENKLE, C.M. (1964), "Warrant prices as indicators of expectations and preferences", in: The random character of stock market prices, edited by P. Cootner, MIT Press, Cambridge, Ma. 1964, 412-474

STOLL, H. (1969), "The relationship between put and call option prices", Journal of Finance, 24, 802-824

STOLL, H. (1973), "The relationship between put and call option prices: reply", Journal of Finance, 28, 185-187

STULZ, R. (1982), "Options on the minimum or the maximum of two risky assets: Analysis and applications", Journal of Financial Economics, 10, 161-185

THORP, E. (1973), "Extensions of the Black-Scholes option model", Bulletin of the International Statistical Institute, Proceedings of the 39th Session, 522-529

UPTON, D. and D. SHANNON (1979), "The stable Paretian distribution, subordinated stochastic processes, and asymptotic lognormality: an empirical investigation", Journal of Finance, 34, 1031-1039

VASICEK, O. (1977), "An equilibrium characterization of the term structure", Journal of Financial Economics, 5, 177-188

Webster's New World Dictionary (1978), edited by D. Guralnik, William Collins + World Publishing Co.

WHALEY, R. (1981), "On the valuation of American call options on stocks with known dividends", Journal of Financial Economics, 9, 207-211

WHALEY, R. (1982), "Valuation of American call options on dividend-paying stocks: empirical tests", Journal of Financial Economics, 10, 29-58

WYMER, C.R. (1972), "Econometric estimation of stochastic differential equation systems", Econometrica, 40, 565-577

A Appendix

A 1 Notation

$\exists$	there exist
$\forall$	for all
$\Rightarrow$	implies
$\Leftrightarrow$	is equivalent
$\vee$	or
$\wedge$	and
$\mathbb{N}$	set of integers
$\mathbb{R}$	set of real numbers
$\mathbb{R}^n$	set of real n-tupels
$\mathbb{R}_+$	set of nonnegative real numbers
$\mathbb{R}_{++}$	set of positive real numbers
$x \in A$ ($x \notin A$)	x is (not) element of the set A
$\emptyset$	empty set
$A \subset B$	A is subset of B
$A \cup B$	union of the sets A and B
$A \cap B$	intersection of the sets A and B
$A \setminus B$; A^c	$:= \{\omega \mid \omega \in A, \omega \notin B\}$; complement of A: $\{\omega \mid \omega \notin A\}$
$A \times B$	cartesian product of the sets A and B
$[a,b]$	closed interval
(a,b)	open interval
1_A	indicator function associated with set A
(Ω, F, P)	probability space
$A(\{F \mid F \in B\})$	σ-algebra generated by B
$A(\{S_s \mid s \leqq t\})$	σ-algebra generated by random variables S_s, $s \leqq t$,
$A \otimes B$	product σ-algebra of A and B
$P_1 \otimes P_2$	product measure of P_1 and P_2
$H_o^{2,c} \oplus H^{2,d}$	direct sum of $H_o^{2,c}$ and $H^{2,d}$
$\gtrsim_a$	preference relation of agent a
$\gg_a$	strict preference relation of agent a
$t \wedge s$	$:= \min(s,t)$
ϕS	$:= \sum_{k=0}^{K} \phi^k S^k$

$\int \phi^k dS^k$	stochastic integral of ϕ^k with respect to S^k
$\int \phi dS$	$:= \sum_{k=0}^{K} \int \phi^k dS^k$
$[S^k,S^k]$	quadratic variation of the semimartingale S^k
$\Vert M \Vert_2$	$:= (E^*[M_T^2])^{1/2}$
$\Vert M \Vert_m$	$:= (E^*[(\sup_{s \leqq T} \vert M_s \vert)^2])^{1/2}$
$\Vert M \Vert_{[,]}$	$:= (E^*[[M,M]_T])^{1/2}$
(c_o,X)	consumption plan
e_a	initial endowment of agent a
$E[X]$	expected value of the random variable X with respect to the basic probability measure P
$E^{P^*}[X]$, $E^*[X]$	expected value of the random variable X with respect to the probability measure P^*
$E[X \vert \mathcal{F}_t]$	conditional expectation
$\mathcal{E}(R)$	(Semimartingale) exponential of the semimartingale R
$\mathbb{F} := (\mathcal{F}_t)_{t \in \mathcal{T}}$	filtration
$\mathcal{H}^2(P^*)$	space of square integrable martingales on $((\Omega,\mathcal{F},P^*),\mathbb{F})$
$\mathcal{H}_o^{2,c}(P^*)$	subspace of $\mathcal{H}^2(P^*)$ consisting of continuous martingales M such that $M_o = 0$ P^* a.s.
$\mathcal{H}^{2,d}(P^*)$	subspace of $\mathcal{H}^2(P^*)$ consisting of purely discontinuous martingales M
$\mathcal{H}_o^{2,d}(P^*)$	subspace of $\mathcal{H}^2(P^*)$ consisting of purely discontinuous martingales M such that $M_o = 0$ a.s.
$\mathcal{L}_{(P^*)}(S^o,\ldots,S^K)$, $\mathcal{L}(P^*)$	stable subspace of $\mathcal{H}^2(P^*)$ generated by $S^o,\ldots,S^K$
$\mathcal{L}(\{N^n \mid n \in \mathbb{N}\})$	closure in $\mathcal{H}^2(P*)$ of the vectorspace $\bigcup_{n \in \mathbb{N}} \mathcal{L}(N^1,\ldots,N^n)$
$(\mathcal{L}(P*))^{\perp}$	strongly orthogonal complement of $\mathcal{L}(P^*)$
$\mathcal{M}_o$	set of feasible consumption plans
$\mathbb{P}(S)$	set of equivalent martingale measures
Φ_o	set of simple selffinancing trading strategies
Φ_{P^*}	set of continuous-time selffinancing trading strategies

$\phi := (\phi^o,\ldots,\phi^K)$	trading strategy
$\lVert \phi \rVert$	$:= \lVert V(\phi) \rVert_m + (E^*[\int_o^T \phi^2 d[S,S]])^{1/2}$
$\lVert \phi \rVert_*$	$:= \lVert V(\phi) \rVert_m + \lVert \int \phi dS \rVert_m$
$\lVert \phi \rVert_m$	$:= (E^*[(\sup_{t \leqq T} \lvert V_t(\phi) \rvert)^2])^{1/2}$
$\lVert \phi \rVert_2$	$:= (E^*[(V_T(\phi))^2])^{1/2}$
Ψ_{P^*} $(\hat{\Psi}_{P^*})$	$:= \{\phi \mid \phi$ predictable, $(V(\phi)$ cadlag$)$, $\lVert \phi \rVert < \infty\}$
$\mathbb{Q}(S)$	set of P-continuous signed martingale measures
$\mathcal{T}$	set of trading dates
$\mathcal{T}(\phi)$	set of trading dates associated with ϕ
S^c	continuous part of the semimartingale S according to the decomposition into continuous and purely discontinuous semimartingales
S^d	purely discontinuous part of the semimartingale S according to the decomposition into continuous and purely discontinuous semimartingales
S^k	price process of security k
$S_t^k(\omega)$	price of security k at time t if the state of the world is ω
S_{t-}	$:= \lim_{s \uparrow t} S_s$
S_-	$:= (S_{t-})_{t \in [O,T]}$
ΔS_t	$:= S_t - S_{t-}$
S_{ω_1}	ω_1-section of S
X	contingent claim
X^+	$:= \max(O,X)$
X^-	$:= \max(O,-X)$
$\mathcal{X}$	space of contingent claims
$\mathcal{X}_+$	$:= \{X \in \mathcal{X} \mid X \geqq O\}$
$\mathcal{X}_{++}$	$:= \{X \in \mathcal{X}_+ \mid E[X] > O\}$
$\mathcal{X}_o$	set of simply attainable contingent claims
$\mathcal{X}_{P^*}$	set of P^*-attainable contingent claims

A 2 Mathematical Tools

A 2.1 Miscellany

(cf. DUNFORD/SCHWARTZ (1957), HILDENBRAND (1974))

Consider the cartesian product $Y \times Y = \{(y_1,y_2) \mid y_1,y_2 \in Y\}$ of the set Y. A subset φ of $Y \times Y$ is called a *binary relation*. It is called

reflexive : $\Leftrightarrow \quad \forall y \in Y : (y,y) \in \varphi$

transitive: $\Leftrightarrow \quad \forall y_1,y_2,y_3 \in Y : (y_1,y_2) \in \varphi \wedge (y_2,y_3) \in \varphi \Rightarrow (y_1,y_3) \in \varphi$

complete : $\Leftrightarrow \quad \forall y_1,y_2 \in Y : (y_1,y_2) \in \varphi \vee (y_2,y_1) \in \varphi$

A *preference relation* is a reflexive, transitive and complete binary relation.

A *metric space* (Y,d_Y) is a nonempty set Y together with a real-valued function $d_Y : Y \times Y \to \mathbb{R}$ such that for all $y_1,y_2,y_3 \in Y$:

(i) $d_Y(y_1,y_2) \geqq 0$, $d_Y(y_1,y_2) = 0 \Leftrightarrow y_1 = y_2$

(ii) $d_Y(y_1,y_2) = d_Y(y_2,y_1)$

(iii) $d_Y(y_1,y_3) \leqq d_Y(y_1,y_2) + d_Y(y_2,y_3)$

A subset G of Y is *open* if for all $y \in G$ there is a positive real number ε such that $B_\varepsilon(y) := \{\tilde{y} \in Y \mid d_Y(y,\tilde{y}) < \varepsilon\} \subset G$. A subset G of Y is *closed* if its complement $G^c := \{y \in Y \mid y \notin G\}$ is an open subset of Y.

A sequence $(y_n)_{n \in \mathbb{N}}$ of elements of Y is a *Cauchy sequence*, if for every $\varepsilon > 0$ there exists $n_o \in \mathbb{N}$ such that $d_Y(y_n,y_m) < \varepsilon$ for all $n,m > n_o$.

A metric space (Y,d_Y) is *complete* if every Cauchy sequence converges to some $y \in Y$.

Let (Y,d_Y) and $(\tilde{Y},d_{\tilde{Y}})$ be metric spaces. A mapping $f: Y \to \tilde{Y}$ is called *isometry*, if for all $y, y' \in Y$

$$d_Y(y,y') = d_{\tilde{Y}}(f(y),f(y'))$$

holds true. (Y,d_Y) and $(\tilde{Y},d_{\tilde{Y}})$ are called *isometric*, if there exists a surjective isometry.

Let Y be a $\mathbb{R}$-vector space. A mapping $\| \cdot \| : Y \to \mathbb{R}$ is called a *norm* on Y if and only if for all $y_1, y_2 \in Y$ and $\lambda \in \mathbb{R}$ the following holds true:

(i) $\| y_1 \| \geqq 0$; $\| y_1 \| = 0 \Leftrightarrow y_1 = 0$

(ii) $\| \lambda y_1 \| = |\lambda| \, \| y_1 \|$

(iii) $\| y_1 + y_2 \| \leqq \| y_1 \| + \| y_2 \|$

$(Y, \| \cdot \|)$ is called a *normed space*. If (i) is replaced by (i')

(i') $\| y_1 \| \geqq 0$,

$\| \cdot \|$ is called a *pseudo-norm* on Y .

Note that a normed space $(Y, \| \cdot \|)$ gives rise to a metric $d_{\| \cdot \|}$ by $d_{\| \cdot \|}(y_1,y_2) := \| y_1 - y_2 \|$. Thus the definitions given above apply to normed spaces. A *Banach space* is a complete normed space.

Two norms $\| \cdot \|_1$ and $\| \cdot \|_2$ on a $\mathbb{R}$-vector space are called *equivalent* if and only if there exists positive real constants c,C such that $c\| y \|_1 \leqq \| y \|_2 \leqq C\| y \|_1$ holds true for all $y \in Y$.

A $\mathbb{R}$-*Hilbert space* $(Y, \langle , \rangle)$ is a $\mathbb{R}$-vector space Y together with a function $\langle , \rangle$ defined on $Y \times Y$ with the properties

(i) $\langle y,y \rangle = 0 \Leftrightarrow y = 0$

(ii) $\langle y,y \rangle \geqq 0 \quad \forall y \in Y$

(iii) $\langle y_1 + y_2, y_3 \rangle = \langle y_1 , y_3 \rangle + \langle y_2 , y_3 \rangle, \ \forall y_1,y_2,y_3 \in Y$

(iv) $\langle \alpha y_1, y_2 \rangle = \alpha \langle y_1, y_2 \rangle, \quad \forall y_1, y_2 \in Y$

(v) $\langle y_1, y_2 \rangle = \langle y_2, y_1 \rangle, \quad \forall y_1, y_2 \in Y$

such that $(Y, \| \cdot \|_{\langle , \rangle})$ is complete, where $\| \cdot \|_{\langle , \rangle}$ is defined by

$$\| y \|_{<,>} := (<y,y>)^{1/2} .$$

$<.,.>$ is called the *scalar* or *inner product* in Y.

A 2.2 Measure Theory

(cf. BAUER (1974), CHOW/TEICHER (1978), DELLACHERIE/MEYER (1978),(1982), HALMOS (1950), METIVIER (1982))

A nonempty class $\mathcal{F}$ of subsets of a set Ω is a *σ-algebra,* if it is closed under the operations of complementation and countable union. $(\Omega,\mathcal{F})$ is called a *measurable space.* If $\mathcal{B}$ is a class of subsets of Ω, the smallest σ-algebra containing $\mathcal{B}$ is the *σ-algebra generated by* $\mathcal{B}$ *(*$\mathcal{A}(\mathcal{B})$*).* Consider two measurable spaces $(\Omega_1,\mathcal{F}_1),(\Omega_2,\mathcal{F}_2)$. The *product σ-algebra* $\mathcal{F}_1 \otimes \mathcal{F}_2$ of $\mathcal{F}_1$ and $\mathcal{F}_2$ is the σ-algebra $\mathcal{A}(\{F_1 \times F_2 | F_1 \in \mathcal{F}_1, F_2 \in \mathcal{F}_2\})$ on $\Omega_1 \times \Omega_2$. If $F \in \mathcal{F}_1 \otimes \mathcal{F}_2$ the ω_1*-sections,* $\omega_1 \in \Omega_1$, and ω_2*-sections,* $\omega_2 \in \Omega_2$, of F, $F_{\omega_1} := \{\omega_2 \in \Omega_2 | (\omega_1,\omega_2) \in F\}$ and

$F_{\omega_2} := \{\omega_1 \in \Omega_1 | (\omega_1,\omega_2) \in F\}$ are elements of $\mathcal{F}_1$ and $\mathcal{F}_2$, respectively. For measurables spaces $(\Omega_1,\mathcal{F}_1)$ and $(\Omega_2,\mathcal{F}_2)$ a mapping $f: \Omega_1 \to \Omega_2$ is $(\mathcal{F}_1 - \mathcal{F}_2)$ *measurable,* if $f^{-1}(F_2) \in \mathcal{F}_1$ for all $F_2 \in \mathcal{F}_2$. f is also called a *random variable.* Consider a family $(\Omega_i,\mathcal{F}_i)_{i\in I}$ of measurable spaces and a family of mappings $(f_i)_{i\in I}$, $f_i : \Omega \to \Omega_i$. The *σ-algebra generated by* $(f_i)_{i\in I}$ $(\mathcal{A}(\{f_i | i \in I\})$ is defined by $\mathcal{A}(\bigcup_{i\in I} \{f_i^{-1}(F_i) | F_i \in \mathcal{F}_i\})$. Consider three measurable spaces $(\Omega_1,\mathcal{F}_1),(\Omega_2,\mathcal{F}_2)$ and $(\Omega_3,\mathcal{F}_3)$. If $f : \Omega_1 \times \Omega_2 \to \Omega_3$ is $\mathcal{F}_1 \otimes \mathcal{F}_2 - \mathcal{F}_3$ measurable, the ω_2*-sections of f* for fixed $\omega_2 \in \Omega_2$

$$f_{\omega_2} : \Omega_1 \to \Omega_3$$
$$\omega_1 \to f(\omega_1,\omega_2)$$

and the ω_1*- sections of f* for fixed $\omega_1 \in \Omega_1$

$$f_{\omega_1} : \Omega_2 \to \Omega_3$$
$$\omega_2 \to f(\omega_1,\omega_2)$$

are $\mathcal{F}_1 - \mathcal{F}_3$ and $\mathcal{F}_2 - \mathcal{F}_3$ measurable, respectively. A *(signed) measure* on a measurable space $(\Omega,\mathcal{F})$ is a mapping $\mu : \mathcal{F} \to \mathbb{R}_+$ $(\mu : \mathcal{F} \to \mathbb{R})$, which is *σ-additive* i.e. for any sequence F_n, $n \in \mathbb{N}$ of pairwise disjoint sets of F $\mu(\bigcup_{n\in\mathbb{N}} F_n) = \sum_{n=1}^{\infty} \mu(F_n)$ holds true. μ is a *probability measure*, if $\mu(\Omega) = 1$ and (Ω,F,μ) is a *probability space*. If X is a real measurable function on a probability space (Ω,F,P), $E[X] := \int X dP$ denotes the expectation of X. If $E[X] < \infty$, X is *integrable*. Let P_1 and P_2 be probability measures on (Ω,F). P_1 is *absolutely continuous with respect to* P_2, $P_1 << P_2$, if for any $F \in F$ we have $P_1(F) = 0$ whenever $P_2(F) = 0$. P_1 and P_2 are *equivalent*, if $P_1 << P_2$ and $P_2 << P_1$ holds true. If $P_1 << P_2$, the *Radon-Nikodym theorem* asserts the existence of a measurable $f : \Omega \to \mathbb{R}_+$ which is unique to within sets of P_2-measure zero, such that $P_1(F) = \int_F f dP_2 \quad \forall F \in F$. f is called the *Radon-Nikodym* derivative of P_1 with respect to P_2 and it is denoted by $\frac{dP_1}{dP_2}$. Let (Ω_1,F_1,P_1) and (Ω_2,F_2,P_2) be two probability spaces. *Fubini's theorem* asserts the existence of a unique probability measure P on $(\Omega_1\times\Omega_2,F_1\otimes F_2)$ such that $P(F_1\times F_2) = P_1(F_1)\,P_2(F_2)$ for all $F_i \in F_i$, i=1,2. P is called the *product measure of* P_1 *and* P_2 and it is denoted by $P_1 \otimes P_2$. Furthermore, for an integrable random variable $f : \Omega_1 \times \Omega_2 \to \mathbb{R}_+$ the following is meaningful and true.

$$\int f d(P_1 \otimes P_2) = \int(\int f_{\omega_1}(\omega_2)dP_2)dP_1 = \int(\int f_{\omega_2}(\omega_1)dP_1)dP_2.$$

Let (Ω,F,P) be a probability space. $L^2 = L^2(\Omega,F,P)$ is the space of square integrable random variables $X : \Omega \to \mathbb{R}$. $\langle X,Y\rangle := E[XY]$ defines a pseudo-inner product, i.e. $\langle .,.\rangle$ has all the properties of an inner product except for $\langle X,X\rangle = 0 \Leftrightarrow X = 0$. However, if one considers the space of equivalence classes of elements of L^2, where X is equivalent to X' iff $P(\{\omega | X(\omega) \neq X'(\omega)\}) = 0$, it becomes a Hilbert space. The induced norm will be denoted by $\| \cdot \|_2$. $L^\infty(\Omega,F,P)$ is the space of random variables $X : \Omega \to \mathbb{R}$ such that X is bounded P almost everywhere.

$\| X \|_\infty := \inf \{c \in \mathbb{R} \mid |X(\omega)| < c \quad \text{a.s.}\}$ is a pseudo -norm on this space. Considering the space of equivalence classes we arrive at a normed space. As usual the same notation will be used for random variables and equivalence classes.

For a probability space (Ω,F,P), a sub-σ-algebra G of F and an integrable random variable X the *conditional expectation of X with respect to G*, $E[X|G]$, is a G-measurable random variable such that $E[1_G\, E[X|G]] = E[1_G\, X]$ for all $G \in G$.

Let (Ω,F,P) be a probability space, T any set and (Y,B) a measurable space. A *stochastic process* defined on Ω, with time set T and state space Y is a family $(S_t)_{t\in T}$ of Y-valued random variables. For every $\omega \in \Omega$, the mapping $t \to S_t(\omega)$ from T into Y is the *path of* ω.

Let $(S_t)_{t\in T}$ and $(S'_t)_{t\in T}$ be two stochastic processes defined on the same probability space (Ω,F,P) with values in the same state space (Y,B). If $S_t = S'_t$ a.s. for each $t \in T$, $(S'_t)_{t\in T}$ is a *modification* of $(S_t)_{t\in T}$. If for almost all $\omega \in \Omega$ $S_t(\omega) = S'_t(\omega)$ for all t, $(S_t)_{t\in T}$ and $(S'_t)_{t\in T}$ are called *indistinguishable*.

From now on we consider the time set $T = [0,T]$, $T \in \mathbb{R}_{++}$. Let (Ω,F) be a measurable space. A *filtration* $\mathbb{F}$ is an increasing family $(F_t)_{t\in[0,T]}$ of sub-σ-algebras of F, i.e. $F_s \subset F_t$ for $s \leqq t$, $s,t \in [0,T]$. $F_{t+} := \bigcap_{s>t} F_s$ defines a filtration $\mathbb{F}_+ := \{F_{t+} | t \in [0,T]\}$. $\mathbb{F}$ is called *right-continuous*, if $F_t = F_{t+}$ for all $t \in [0,T]$. $\mathbb{F}$ is called *complete*, if $\tilde{F} \in F_t$ for all $t \in [0,T]$, whenever $\tilde{F} \subset F \in F$ such that $P(F) = 0$. $\mathbb{F}$ is said to satisfy the *usual conditions*, if it is complete and right-continuous. It is always possible to arrive at a filtration satisfying the usual conditions. An arbitrary filtration can always be completed: one completes the space (Ω,G,P) yielding $(\Omega,\tilde{G},\tilde{P})$ and then adjoins to each σ-algebra $\{N \subset \Omega | N$ is $\tilde{P}$ null set$\}$. If this operation is performed on the family made right-continuous via $G_t := F_{t+}$, one gets a family (I_t), which satisfies the usual conditions and which is called the *usual augmentation* of the family (F_t).

Let (Ω,F,P) be a probability space and $(F_t)_{t\in[0,T]}$ a filtration. A mapping $\tau: \Omega \to [0,T]$ is a *stopping-time*, if $\{\tau \leqq t\} \in F_t$ for all $t \in [0,T]$. For two stopping times such that $\tau_1 \leqq \tau_2$ a.s. *stochastic intervals* $]\tau_1,\tau_2]$, $[\tau_1,\tau_2]$, $[\tau_1,\tau_2[$ and $]\tau_1,\tau_2[$ are defined by

$$]\tau_1,\tau_2] := \{(t,\omega) \in [0,T] \times \Omega | \tau_1(\omega) < t \leqq \tau_2(\omega)\}$$

$$[\tau_1,\tau_2] := \{(t,\omega) \in [0,T] \times \Omega | \tau_1(\omega) \leqq t \leqq \tau_2(\omega)\}$$

$$[\tau_1,\tau_2[:= \{(t,\omega) \in [0,T] \times \Omega | \tau_1(\omega) \leqq t < \tau_2(\omega)\}$$

$$]\tau_1,\tau_2[:= \{(t,\omega) \in [0,T] \times \Omega | \tau_1(\omega) < t < \tau_2(\omega)\}$$

Let $S = (S_t)_{t\in[0,T]}$ be a stochastic process defined on a measurable space (Ω,F) and let $\mathbb{F} := (F_t)_{t\in[0,T]}$ be a filtration. S is *adapted to* $\mathbb{F}$, if S_t is F_t-measurable for every $t \in [0,T]$. S is *cadlag* (continue à droite limites a gauche), if S has paths that are right-continuous on $[0,T]$ and have left limits on $(0,T]$. Left limits of S are denoted by S_-. If S is cadlag, $\Delta S_t := S_t - S_{t-}$ defines the *jump of S* at time t. S is *continuous*, if S has continuous paths on $(0,T]$. The σ-algebra on $[0,T] \times \Omega$ generated by the real, adapted and continuous processes is called the *predictable σ-algebra*. A process H is *predictable*, if the

function $(t,\omega) \to H_t(\omega)$ on $[0,T] \times \Omega$ is measurable with respect to the predictable σ-algebra and the Borel σ-algebra on $\mathbb{R}$. A predictable process H is *locally bounded* if there exist stopping times $T_n \uparrow T$ and constants c_n such that $|H - H_0|$ is bounded above by c_n on $[0,T_n]$. A stochastic process S has the *elementary Markov-property* if for every $B \in \mathcal{B}$ and all $s,t \in [0,T]$ such that $s < t$
$P(\{S_t \in B|\mathcal{A}(\{S_r|r \leq s\})\}) = P(\{S_t \in B|\mathcal{A}(\{S_s\})\})$ a.s.

From now on we consider a given probability space $(\Omega,\mathcal{F},P)$ with a filtration $\mathbb{F} := (\mathcal{F}_t)_{t\in[0,T]}$ satisfying the usual conditions and an adapted cadlag process $S = (S_t)_{t\in[0,T]}$. S is a *martingale with respect to* $\mathbb{F}$, if each S_t is integrable and $E[S_t|\mathcal{F}_s] = S_s$ holds true a.s. for $s \leq t$, $s,t \in [0,T]$. S is a *local martingale* (with respect to $\mathbb{F}$) if there exists an increasing sequence of stopping times T_n of $\mathbb{F}$ such that $\lim_n T_n = T$ a.s. and the processes $S_{t\wedge T_n} I_{\{T_n>0\}}$ are all integrable martingales. A process S is a *semimartingale* of $\mathbb{F}$ if it has a decomposition $S_t = S_0 + M_t + A_t$ where M is a local martingale which is zero at 0 and A is a right-continuous adapted process which is zero at 0 and whose paths are of finite variation. The semimartingale is *special* if there exists a decomposition of the form given above for which A is predictable. With a P-integrable random variable X we associate the cadlag modification of $(E^*[X|\mathcal{F}_t])$ and denote it by (X_t). Note that if (Y_t) is a modification of (X_t) and both processes are right-continuous, then (X_t) and (Y_t) are indistinguishable. (cf. ELLOTT (1982), Lemma 2.21, p.13)

An *n-dimensional Brownian motion* with respect to $((\Omega,\mathcal{F},P),(\mathcal{F}_t)_{t\in[0,T]})$ is a stochastic process S with state space $(\mathbb{R}^n,\mathcal{B}^n)$ and the following properties:

(i) $S_0 = 0$ a.s.

(ii) S has *increments independent of the past*, i.e. for all $s,t \in [0,T]$ such that $s < t$, the random variable $S_t - S_s$ is independent of the σ-algebra $\mathcal{F}_s$.

(iii) for all $s,t \in [0,T]$ such that $s < t$, $X_t - X_s$ is a Gaussian random variable with mean μ and variance matrix $(t - s)C$, where C is a given matrix.

S is a *standard n-dimensional Brownian motion* if $\mu = 0$ and C is the identity matrix. Note that S can be chosen to have continuous paths, which is called the *canonical Brownian motion*. If $n = 1$, we refer to this process as *Brownian motion*. A *geometric Brownian motion* is a stochastic process S defined by

$$\ln S_t = \sigma W_t + \mu t + a \qquad \text{for all } t \in [0,T],$$

where σ, a, μ are constants and W is a standard Brownian motion.
A *Poisson process with parameter* $\lambda > 0$ with respect to $((\Omega,F,P),(F_t)_{t\in[0,T]})$ is a stochastic process S with state space $\mathbb{N}$ and the following properties:

(i) $N_0 = 0$ a.s.

(ii) N has increments independent of the past.

(iii) for all $s,t \in [0,T]$ such that $s < t$, $N_t - N_s$ is a Poisson random variable with parameter $(t - s)\lambda$ (i.e. $P(\{N_t - N_s = k\}) = \exp(-\lambda(t-s))\frac{\lambda^k (t-s)^k}{k!})$.

A *geometric Poisson process* is a stochastic process S defined by

$$\ln S_t = N_t + b\,t + a \qquad \text{for all } t \in [0,T],$$

where a and b are constants and N is a Poisson process.
A *stable distribution* is described by the associated characteristic function of the form

$$\varphi(t) = \exp\{i\gamma t - c|t|^\alpha (1 + i\beta\frac{t}{|t|} w(t,\alpha))\}$$

where $0 < \alpha \leq 2$, $|\beta| \leq 1$, $c \geq 0$, $\gamma > 0$ and $w(t,\alpha) = \begin{cases} \tan \pi\alpha/2 & \alpha \neq 1 \\ (2/\pi)\log|t| & \alpha = 1 \end{cases}$

If $\alpha = 2$ (and necessarily $\beta = 0$), the normal characteristic function results. If $\alpha = 1$, $\gamma = 0$ and $c = 1$, this yields a Cauchy characteristic function. A stable distribution is *symmetric*, if $\beta = \gamma = 0$ holds true for the associated characteristic function. Note that the class of stable distributions is the class of limit distributions of normed sums of i.i.d. random variables.
A *Student distribution* is described by a density of the form

$$f(x) = \frac{\Gamma(m)}{\Gamma(\frac{1}{2})\,\Gamma(m - \frac{1}{2})\,(1 + x^2)^m}$$

for $m \geq 1$, $-\infty \leq x \leq +\infty$

A 2.3 Stochastic calculus

(cf. DELLACHERIE/MEYER(1978),(1982),JACOD(1979),ELLIOTT(1982))

Let (Ω,F,P) be a probability space and $\mathbb{F} := (F_t)_{t\in[0,T]}$ a filtration that satisfies the usual conditions. $H^2(P)$ denotes the space of square-integrable martingales on $((\Omega,F,P),\mathbb{F})$. We identify martingales that are indistinguishable. As in the case of L^p spaces, we use the same notation for the resulting space of equivalence classes. $H^2(P)$ is a Banach space with the norm $\| \ \|_m$ defined by

$$\| M \|_m := (E[(\sup_{t\leq T}|M_t|)^2])^{1/2}.$$

$H^2(P)$ can be identified with the Hilbert space $L^2(\Omega,F,P)$ by identifying a square-integrable martingale with its random variable at time T. Thus $H^2(P)$ becomes a Hilbert space with the inner product $\langle\langle M^1,M^2\rangle\rangle := E[M_T^1 \, M_T^2]$. The corresponding norm is denoted by $\| \ \|_2$, i.e.

$$\| M \|_2 := (E[M_T^2])^{1/2}.$$

$\| \ \|_m$ and $\| \ \|_2$ are equivalent norms on $H^2(P^*)$.

Two square integrable martingales M^1 and M^2 are called *strongly orthogonal* if $M^1 \, M^2$ is a martingale which is zero at 0. Strong orthogonality implies orthogonality in the Hilbert space sense, i.e. if M^1 and M^2 are strongly orthogonal $E[M_T^1 \, M_T^2] = 0$ holds true. A subspace K of $H^2(P)$ is called *stable* iff

(i) K is closed in the L^2 norm topology

(ii) K is closed with respect to stopping, i.e. for every stopping time τ and $M \in K$, $M^\tau \in K$

(iii) If $M \in K$ and $A \in F_0$, then $1_A M \in K$.

If K is stable,
$K^\perp := \{N \in H^2(P) \,|\, E[M_T N_T] = 0 \quad \forall \, M \in K\}$ is a stable subspace. If $M \in K$ and $N \in K^\perp$, then M and N are strongly orthogonal.

Suppose K is a stable subspace of $H^2(P)$. Then every element $M \in H^2(P)$ has a unique decomposition

$$M = N + N'$$

where $N \in K$ and $N' \in K^{\perp}$.

$H_0^{2,c}(P)$ is the space of continuous square integrable martingales, which are zero at 0. $H_0^{2,c}(P)$ is a stable subspace of $H^2(P)$. $H^{2,d}(P)$ denotes the space $(H_0^{2,c}(P))^{\perp}$ and elements of $H^{2,d}(P)$ are said to be *purely discontinuous*. For $M \in H^2(P)$ consider the unique decomposition into a continuous martingale, which is zero at 0, and a purely discontinuous martingale. The continuous martingale part of M and the purely discontinuous martingale part of M will be denoted by M^c and M^d, respectively.

For any element $M \in H^2(P)$ the Doob-Meyer decomposition of M^2 implies the existence of a unique predictable process $\langle M,M\rangle$ with paths that are right-continuous and increasing such that $M^2 - \langle M,M\rangle$ is a martingale, which is zero at 0. $\langle M,M\rangle$ is called the *predictable quadratic variation of* M. For $M \in H^2(P)$ an increasing process $[M,M]$ is defined by

$$[M,M]_t := \langle M^c,M^c\rangle_t + \sum_{s \leqq t} \Delta M_s^2 \quad ,$$

for $t \in [0,T]$. $[M,M]$ is called the *(optional) quadratic variation of* M. Suppose $M,N \in H^2(P)$. The processes $\langle M,N\rangle$ and $[M,N]$ are defined by polarisation, i.e.

$$\langle M,N\rangle := \frac{1}{2}(\langle M + N,M + N\rangle - \langle M,M\rangle - \langle N,N\rangle)$$

$$[M,N] := \frac{1}{2}([M + N,M + N] - [M,M] - [N,N])$$

Note that $\| \quad \|_{[,]}$ given by

$$\| M \|_{[,]} := (E[M,M]_T)^{1/2}$$

defines a norm on $H^2(P)$, which is equivalent to $\| \quad \|_2$. The concepts introduced so far can all be extended to semimartingales in an obvious way. The corresponding semimartingale concepts will also be considered in what follows.

For $S^k \in H^2(P)$ let $L_P^2(S^k)$ be the space L^2 of the measure associated with the integrable increasing process $\langle S^k,S^k\rangle$ over the predictable σ-algebra. For a predictable process ϕ^k of the form (3.1.9) the *stochastic integral with respect to* S^k, denoted by $\int\phi dS^k$, is defined by

$$\int_0^t \phi^k \, dS^k := \phi^k_{-1} \, S^k_0 + \sum_{i=1}^{N} \phi^k_{i-1} \, (S^k_{t_i \wedge t} - S^k_{t_{i-1} \wedge t}) \qquad t \in [0,T].$$

Quite often $\int \phi^k dS^k$ is also denoted $\int \phi^k_s \, dS^k_s$. The mapping $\phi^k \to \int \phi^k \, dS^k$ maps the set of simple predictable processes isometrically into $H^2(P)$ and can be extended uniquely to an isometry of $L^2_P(S^k)$ into $H^2(P)$ (also denoted by $\phi^k \to \int \phi^k \, dS^k$ and called *stochastic integral*). The restriction of this isometry to locally bounded predictable processes has the following properties:
If ϕ^k and ψ^k are locally bounded and predictable, then

$$\int \phi^k \, d(\int \psi^k \, dS^k) = \int \phi^k \, \psi^k \, dS^k \quad .$$

The jumps of $\int \phi^k \, dS^k$ are given by

$$\Delta(\int \phi^k \, dS^k) = \phi^k \, \Delta S^k \quad .$$

The concept of the stochastic integral can be extended to semimartingales S^k. Let S^k be a semimartingale. Then as above, the mapping $\phi^k \to \int \phi^k \, dS^k$ on the set of simple predictable processes has a unique extension to the space of all locally bounded predictable processes, which is linear in ϕ^k and such that $\int \phi^k \, dS^k$ is a semimartingale. The stochastic integral has the properties as stated above. Furthermore

$$[\int \phi^k \, dS^k, S^l] = \int \phi^k \, d[S^k, S^l]$$

for semimartingales S^k and S^l and ϕ^k a locally bounded predictable process.

Let $S^1, \ldots, S^K$ be real-valued semimartingales and let f be a twice continuously differentiable function on $\mathbb{R}^n$. *Ito's lemma* asserts that $f(S^1, \ldots, S^K)$ is a semimartingale. In particular,

$$f(S_t^1,\ldots,S_t^K) = f(S_0^1,\ldots,S_0^K)$$

$$+ \sum_{k=1}^{K} \int_0^t \left(\frac{\partial f}{\partial S^k}\right)_- dS^k + \frac{1}{2} \sum_{k,l=1}^{K} \int_0^t \left(\frac{\partial^2 f}{\partial S^k \partial S^l}\right)_- d[S^k,S^l]^c$$

$$+ \sum_{0<s\leqq t} (f(S_s^1,\ldots,S_s^K) - f(S_{s-}^1,\ldots,S_{s-}^K)$$

$$- \sum_{k=1}^{K} \left(\frac{\partial f}{\partial S^k}\right)_{s-} \Delta S_s^k)) \ ,$$

for all $t \in [0,T]$, where $[S^k,S^l]^c$ denotes the continuous part of the semimartingale $[S^k,S^l]$, and equality denotes indistinguishability.

If $S^1,\ldots,S^K$ are continuous processes this reduces to

$$f(S_t^1,\ldots,S_t^K) = f(S_0^1,\ldots,S_0^K) + \sum_{k=1}^{K} \int_0^t \left(\frac{\partial f}{\partial S^k}\right)_- dS^k$$

$$+ \frac{1}{2} \sum_{k,l=1}^{K} \int_0^t \left(\frac{\partial^2 f}{\partial S^k \partial S^l}\right)_- d[S^k,S^l]$$

for all $t \in [0,T]$.

For the product S^1S^2 of two semimartingales S^1 and S^2 Ito's lemma reduces to

$$S_t^1 S_t^2 = \int_0^t S_-^1 \, dS^2 + \int_0^t S_-^2 \, dS^1 + [S^1,S^2]_t$$

for all $t \in [0,T]$.

Suppose R is a semimartingale. Then there is a unique semimartingale S such that

$$S_t = S_0 + \int_0^t S_- \, dR$$

holds true for all $t \in [0,T]$. S is called the *exponential of* R and it is denoted by $S = S_0\mathcal{E}(R)$. S is given by

$$S_t = S_0 \exp(R_t - R_0 - \tfrac{1}{2}[R^c,R^c]_t) \prod_{0<s\leq t} ((1 + \Delta R_s) \exp(-\Delta R_s))$$

for all $t \in [0,T]$, where the infinite product is absolutely convergent almost surely.

Index

Vol. 157: Optimization and Operations Research. Proceedings 1977. Edited by R. Henn, B. Korte, and W. Oettli. VI, 270 pages. 1978.

Vol. 158: L. J. Cherene, Set Valued Dynamical Systems and Economic Flow. VIII, 83 pages. 1978.

Vol. 159: Some Aspects of the Foundations of General Equilibrium Theory: The Posthumous Papers of Peter J. Kalman. Edited by J. Green. VI, 167 pages. 1978.

Vol. 160: Integer Programming and Related Areas. A Classified Bibliography. Edited by D. Hausmann. XIV, 314 pages. 1978.

Vol. 161: M. J. Beckmann, Rank in Organizations. VIII, 164 pages. 1978.

Vol. 162: Recent Developments in Variable Structure Systems, Economics and Biology. Proceedings 1977. Edited by R. R. Mohler and A. Ruberti. VI, 326 pages. 1978.

Vol. 163: G. Fandel, Optimale Entscheidungen in Organisationen. VI, 143 Seiten. 1979.

Vol. 164: C. L. Hwang and A. S. M. Masud, Multiple Objective Decision Making – Methods and Applications. A State-of-the-Art Survey. XII, 351 pages. 1979.

Vol. 165: A. Maravall, Identification in Dynamic Shock-Error Models. VIII, 158 pages. 1979.

Vol. 166: R. Cuninghame-Green, Minimax Algebra. XI, 258 pages. 1979.

Vol. 167: M. Faber, Introduction to Modern Austrian Capital Theory. X, 196 pages. 1979.

Vol. 168: Convex Analysis and Mathematical Economics. Proceedings 1978. Edited by J. Kriens. V, 136 pages. 1979.

Vol. 169: A. Rapoport et al., Coalition Formation by Sophisticated Players. VII, 170 pages. 1979.

Vol. 170: A. E. Roth, Axiomatic Models of Bargaining. V, 121 pages. 1979.

Vol. 171: G. F. Newell, Approximate Behavior of Tandem Queues. XI, 410 pages. 1979.

Vol. 172: K. Neumann and U. Steinhardt, GERT Networks and the Time-Oriented Evaluation of Projects. 268 pages. 1979.

Vol. 173: S. Erlander, Optimal Spatial Interaction and the Gravity Model. VII, 107 pages. 1980.

Vol. 174: Extremal Methods and Systems Analysis. Edited by A. V. Fiacco and K. O. Kortanek. XI, 545 pages. 1980.

Vol. 175: S. K. Srinivasan and R. Subramanian, Probabilistic Analysis of Redundant Systems. VII, 356 pages. 1980.

Vol. 176: R. Färe, Laws of Diminishing Returns. VIII, 97 pages. 1980.

Vol. 177: Multiple Criteria Decision Making-Theory and Application. Proceedings, 1979. Edited by G. Fandel and T. Gal. XVI, 570 pages. 1980.

Vol. 178: M. N. Bhattacharyya, Comparison of Box-Jenkins and Bonn Monetary Model Prediction Performance. VII, 146 pages. 1980.

Vol. 179: Recent Results in Stochastic Programming. Proceedings, 1979. Edited by P. Kall and A. Prékopa. IX, 237 pages. 1980.

Vol. 180: J. F. Brotchie, J. W. Dickey and R. Sharpe, TOPAZ – General Planning Technique and its Applications at the Regional, Urban, and Facility Planning Levels. VII, 356 pages. 1980.

Vol. 181: H. D. Sherali and C. M. Shetty, Optimization with Disjunctive Constraints. VIII, 156 pages. 1980.

Vol. 182: J. Wolters, Stochastic Dynamic Properties of Linear Econometric Models. VIII, 154 pages. 1980.

Vol. 183: K. Schittkowski, Nonlinear Programming Codes. VIII, 242 pages. 1980.

Vol. 184: R. E. Burkard and U. Derigs, Assignment and Matching Problems: Solution Methods with FORTRAN-Programs. VIII, 148 pages. 1980.

Vol. 185: C. C. von Weizsäcker, Barriers to Entry. VI, 220 pages. 1980.

Vol. 186: Ch.-L. Hwang and K. Yoon, Multiple Attribute Decision Making – Methods and Applications. A State-of-the-Art-Survey. XI, 259 pages. 1981.

Vol. 187: W. Hock, K. Schittkowski, Test Examples for Nonlinear Programming Codes. V. 178 pages. 1981.

Vol. 188: D. Bös, Economic Theory of Public Enterprise. VII, 142 pages. 1981.

Vol. 189: A. P. Lüthi, Messung wirtschaftlicher Ungleichheit. IX, 287 pages. 1981.

Vol. 190: J. N. Morse, Organizations: Multiple Agents with Multiple Criteria. Proceedings, 1980. VI, 509 pages. 1981.

Vol. 191: H. R. Sneessens, Theory and Estimation of Macroeconomic Rationing Models. VII, 138 pages. 1981.

Vol. 192: H. J. Bierens: Robust Methods and Asymptotic Theory in Nonlinear Econometrics. IX, 198 pages. 1981.

Vol. 193: J.K. Sengupta, Optimal Decisions under Uncertainty. VII, 156 pages. 1981.

Vol. 194: R. W. Shephard, Cost and Production Functions. XI, 104 pages. 1981.

Vol. 195: H. W. Ursprung, Die elementare Katastrophentheorie. Eine Darstellung aus der Sicht der Ökonomie. VII, 332 pages. 1982.

Vol. 196: M. Nermuth, Information Structures in Economics. VIII, 236 pages. 1982.

Vol. 197: Integer Programming and Related Areas. A Classified Bibliography. 1978 – 1981. Edited by R. von Randow. XIV, 338 pages. 1982.

Vol. 198: P. Zweifel, Ein ökonomisches Modell des Arztverhaltens. XIX, 392 Seiten. 1982.

Vol. 199: Evaluating Mathematical Programming Techniques. Proceedings, 1981. Edited by J.M. Mulvey. XI, 379 pages. 1982.

Vol. 200: The Resource Sector in an Open Economy. Edited by H. Siebert. IX, 161 pages. 1984.

Vol. 201: P. M. C. de Boer, Price Effects in Input-Output-Relations: A Theoretical and Empirical Study for the Netherlands 1949–1967. X, 140 pages. 1982.

Vol. 202: U. Witt, J. Perske, SMS – A Program Package for Simulation and Gaming of Stochastic Market Processes and Learning Behavior. VII, 266 pages. 1982.

Vol. 203: Compilation of Input-Output Tables. Proceedings, 1981. Edited by J. V. Skolka. VII, 307 pages. 1982.

Vol. 204: K.C. Mosler, Entscheidungsregeln bei Risiko: Multivariate stochastische Dominanz. VII, 172 Seiten. 1982.

Vol. 205: R. Ramanathan, Introduction to the Theory of Economic Growth. IX, 347 pages. 1982.

Vol. 206: M.H. Karwan, V. Lotfi, J. Telgen, and S. Zionts, Redundancy in Mathematical Programming. VII, 286 pages. 1983.

Vol. 207: Y. Fujimori, Modern Analysis of Value Theory. X, 165 pages. 1982.

Vol. 208: Econometric Decision Models. Proceedings, 1981. Edited by J. Gruber. VI, 364 pages. 1983.

Vol. 209: Essays and Surveys on Multiple Criteria Decision Making. Proceedings, 1982. Edited by P. Hansen. VII, 441 pages. 1983.

Vol. 210: Technology, Organization and Economic Structure. Edited by R. Sato and M.J. Beckmann. VIII, 195 pages. 1983.

Vol. 211: P. van den Heuvel, The Stability of a Macroeconomic System with Quantity Constraints. VII, 169 pages. 1983.

Vol. 212: R. Sato and T. Nôno, Invariance Principles and the Structure of Technology. V, 94 pages. 1983.

Vol. 213: Aspiration Levels in Bargaining and Economic Decision Making. Proceedings, 1982. Edited by R. Tietz. VIII, 406 pages. 1983.

Vol. 214: M. Faber, H. Niemes und G. Stephan, Entropie, Umweltschutz und Rohstoffverbrauch. IX, 181 Seiten. 1983.

Vol. 215: Semi-Infinite Programming and Applications. Proceedings, 1981. Edited by A.V. Fiacco and K.O. Kortanek. XI, 322 pages. 1983.

Vol. 216: H.H. Müller, Fiscal Policies in a General Equilibrium Model with Persistent Unemployment. VI, 92 pages. 1983.

Vol. 217: Ch. Grootaert, The Relation Between Final Demand and Income Distribution. XIV, 105 pages. 1983.

Vol. 218: P. van Loon, A Dynamic Theory of the Firm: Production, Finance and Investment. VII, 191 pages. 1983.

Vol. 219: E. van Damme, Refinements of the Nash Equilibrium Concept. VI, 151 pages. 1983.

Vol. 220: M. Aoki, Notes on Economic Time Series Analysis: System Theoretic Perspectives. IX, 249 pages. 1983.

Vol. 221: S. Nakamura, An Inter-Industry Translog Model of Prices and Technical Change for the West German Economy. XIV, 290 pages. 1984.

Vol. 222: P. Meier, Energy Systems Analysis for Developing Countries. VI, 344 pages. 1984.

Vol. 223: W. Trockel, Market Demand. VIII, 205 pages. 1984.

Vol. 224: M. Kiy, Ein disaggregiertes Prognosesystem für die Bundesrepublik Deutschland. XVIII, 276 Seiten. 1984.

Vol. 225: T.R. von Ungern-Sternberg, Zur Analyse von Märkten mit unvollständiger Nachfragerinformation. IX, 125 Seiten. 1984

Vol. 226: Selected Topics in Operations Research and Mathematical Economics. Proceedings, 1983. Edited by G. Hammer and D. Pallaschke. IX, 478 pages. 1984.

Vol. 227: Risk and Capital. Proceedings, 1983. Edited by G. Bamberg and K. Spremann. VII, 306 pages. 1984.

Vol. 228: Nonlinear Models of Fluctuating Growth. Proceedings, 1983. Edited by R.M. Goodwin, M. Krüger and A. Vercelli. XVII, 277 pages. 1984.

Vol. 229: Interactive Decision Analysis. Proceedings, 1983. Edited by M. Grauer and A.P. Wierzbicki. VIII, 269 pages. 1984.

Vol. 230: Macro-Economic Planning with Conflicting Goals. Proceedings, 1982. Edited by M. Despontin, P. Nijkamp and J. Spronk. VI, 297 pages. 1984.

Vol. 231: G.F. Newell, The M/M/∞ Service System with Ranked Servers in Heavy Traffic. XI, 126 pages. 1984.

Vol. 232: L. Bauwens, Bayesian Full Information Analysis of Simultaneous Equation Models Using Integration by Monte Carlo. VI, 114 pages. 1984.

Vol. 233: G. Wagenhals, The World Copper Market. XI, 190 pages. 1984.

Vol. 234: B.C. Eaves, A Course in Triangulations for Solving Equations with Deformations. III, 302 pages. 1984.

Vol. 235: Stochastic Models in Reliability Theory. Proceedings, 1984. Edited by S. Osaki and Y. Hatoyama. VII, 212 pages. 1984.

Vol. 236: G. Gandolfo, P.C. Padoan, A Disequilibrium Model of Real and Financial Accumulation in an Open Economy. VI, 172 pages. 1984.

Vol. 237: Misspecification Analysis. Proceedings, 1983. Edited by T.K. Dijkstra. V, 129 pages. 1984.

Vol. 238: W. Domschke, A. Drexl, Location and Layout Planning. IV, 134 pages. 1985.

Vol. 239: Microeconomic Models of Housing Markets. Edited by K. Stahl. VII, 197 pages. 1985.

Vol. 240: Contributions to Operations Research. Proceedings, 1984. Edited by K. Neumann and D. Pallaschke. V, 190 pages. 1985.

Vol. 241: U. Wittmann, Das Konzept rationaler Preiserwartungen. XI, 310 Seiten. 1985.

Vol. 242: Decision Making with Multiple Objectives. Proceedings, 1984. Edited by Y.Y. Haimes and V. Chankong. XI, 571 pages. 1985.

Vol. 243: Integer Programming and Related Areas. A Classified Bibliography 1981–1984. Edited by R. von Randow. XX, 386 pages. 1985.

Vol. 244: Advances in Equilibrium Theory. Proceedings, 1984. Edited by C.D. Aliprantis, O. Burkinshaw and N.J. Rothman. II, 235 pages. 1985.

Vol. 245: J.E.M. Wilhelm, Arbitrage Theory. VII, 114 pages. 1985.

Vol. 246: P.W. Otter, Dynamic Feature Space Modelling, Filtering and Self-Tuning Control of Stochastic Systems. XIV, 177 pages. 1985.

Vol. 247: Optimization and Discrete Choice in Urban Systems. Proceedings, 1983. Edited by B.G. Hutchinson, P. Nijkamp and M. Batty. VI, 371 pages. 1985.

Vol. 248: Plural Rationality and Interactive Decision Processes. Proceedings, 1984. Edited by M. Grauer, M. Thompson and A.P. Wierzbicki. VI, 354 pages. 1985.

Vol. 249: Spatial Price Equilibrium: Advances in Theory, Computation and Application. Proceedings, 1984. Edited by P. T. Harker. VII, 277 pages. 1985.

Vol. 250: M. Roubens, Ph. Vincke, Preference Modelling. VIII, 94 pages. 1985.

Vol. 251: Input-Output Modeling. Proceedings, 1984. Edited by A. Smyshlyaev. VI, 261 pages. 1985.

Vol. 252: A. Birolini, On the Use of Stochastic Processes in Modeling Reliability Problems. VI, 105 pages. 1985.

Vol. 253: C. Withagen, Economic Theory and International Trade in Natural Exhaustible Resources. VI, 172 pages. 1985.

Vol. 254: S. Müller, Arbitrage Pricing of Contingent Claims. VIII, 151 pages. 1985.

GPSR Compliance

The European Union's (EU) General Product Safety Regulation (GPSR) is a set of rules that requires consumer products to be safe and our obligations to ensure this.

If you have any concerns about our products, you can contact us on ProductSafety@springernature.com

In case Publisher is established outside the EU, the EU authorized representative is:

Springer Nature Customer Service Center GmbH
Europaplatz 3
69115 Heidelberg, Germany

Batch number: 10844827

Printed by Printforce, the Netherlands